My Motorola
Xoom™

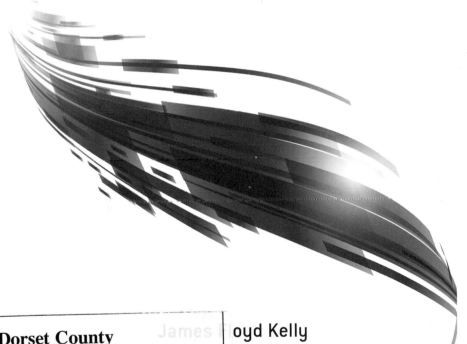

James Floyd Kelly

que®

800 East 96th Street,
Indianapolis, Indiana 46240 USA

My Motorola Xoom™

Copyright © 2012 by Pearson Education

ISBN-13: 978-0-7897-4826-3
ISBN-10: 0-7897-4826-6

The Library of Congress cataloging-in-publication data is on file.

Printed in the United States of America

First Printing: July 2011

Trademarks

Warning and Disclaimer

Bulk Sales

Que Publishing offers excellent discounts on this book when ordered in quantity for bulk purchases or special sales. For more information, please contact

U.S. Corporate and Government Sales
1-800-382-3419
corpsales@pearsontechgroup.com

For sales outside of the U.S., please contact

International Sales
international@pearson.com

PUBLISHER
Paul Boger

ASSOCIATE PUBLISHER
Greg Wiegand

ACQUISITIONS EDITOR
Laura Norman

DEVELOPMENT EDITOR
The Wordsmithery LLC

MANAGING EDITOR
Kristy Hart

PROJECT EDITOR
Jovana San Nicolas-Shirley

COPY EDITOR
Sheri Cain

INDEXER
Cheryl Lenser

PROOFREADER
Seth Kerney

PUBLISHING COORDINATOR
Cindy Teeters

COVER DESIGNER
Anne Jones

COMPOSITOR
Nonie Ratcliff

Table of Contents

About the Author

James Floyd Kelly is the author of *Sams Teach Yourself Galaxy Tab in 10 Minutes,* and a writer and blogger from Atlanta, Georgia. He has a B.A. in English (University of West Florida) and B.S. in Industrial Engineering (Florida State University). He has worked in technology for more than 15 years, including work as a technical trainer, network systems administrator, and technology outsourcing consultant.

Jim has written books and articles on numerous other subjects, including building a CNC machine, programming and building robots, using open source software, video editing with Movie Maker Live, and building an Ubuntu Linux PC.

Jim is the editor-in-chief of the most popular LEGO MINDSTORMS NXT robotics blog, The NXT Step (www.thenxtstep.com), and he provides robot building and programming training and coaching to local teachers and students.

Dedication

For Decker: Yes, you can play Angry Birds on it.

Acknowledgments

I really enjoy writing for Pearson, and I have to thank Laura Norman for all of her help and answers regarding the *My* book series. Laura and the rest of the team at Pearson publish great books, and I appreciate every chance I can to contribute.

A special thanks also goes to my good friend, David Levy, who offered to serve as technical editor and purchased his own Xoom so he could follow along and verify all the steps.

We Want to Hear from You!

As the reader of this book, *you* are our most important critic and commentator. We value your opinion and want to know what we're doing right, what we could do better, what areas you'd like to see us publish in, and any other words of wisdom you're willing to pass our way.

As an associate publisher for Que Publishing, I welcome your comments. You can email or write me directly to let me know what you did or didn't like about this book—as well as what we can do to make our books better.

Please note that I cannot help you with technical problems related to the topic of this book. We do have a User Services group, however, where I will forward specific technical questions related to the book.

When you write, please be sure to include this book's title and author as well as your name, email address, and phone number. I will carefully review your comments and share them with the author and editors who worked on the book.

Email: feedback@quepublishing.com

Mail: Greg Wiegand
Associate Publisher
Que Publishing
800 East 96th Street
Indianapolis, IN 46240 USA

Reader Services

Visit our website and register this book at quepublishing.com/register for convenient access to any updates, downloads, or errata that might be available for this book.

Learn how to use the new Android operating system, Honeycomb, and its newly redesigned user interface.

In this chapter, you learn about the Xoom's touch screen, user interface, and the device's various buttons and ports.

Getting Started

The Xoom is a touch screen tablet, meaning that most every task you perform with it involves using the touch-sensitive screen. Opening apps, moving items, enlarging pictures, and other tasks all involve moving a finger (or fingers) on the screen. However, some actions you perform involve buttons or features that are included on the Xoom's outer shell. In this chapter, you learn all about the Xoom's user interface, how to properly use the touch screen, and what features are available on the Xoom's shell.

Xoom Shell

The Xoom features a Power/Lock button, two volume control buttons (increase/decrease buttons), two speakers, a webcam, a digital camera, a headphone jack, a micro SD card slot, a charging port, a micro USB port, and an HDMI port.

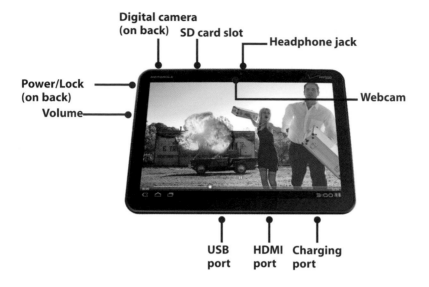

Digital camera
(on back)   SD card slot
                                    Headphone jack

Power/Lock
(on back)
Volume

Webcam

USB   HDMI   Charging
port   port   port

Power/Lock Button

The Power/Lock button serves two purposes. The first is a simple On/Off switch that puts your Xoom into Sleep Mode. Sleep Mode doesn't completely turn off the Xoom, and while the Xoom sleeps, it continues to draw power from the battery, although it does so at a slower rate than when it is on. Quickly pressing and releasing the button locks the Xoom and protects the touch screen from accidental usage.

The second function of the Power/Lock button is to completely turn off the Xoom. Pressing and holding the Power/Lock button displays a window asking if you want to shut down the device. Press OK to completely power down the Xoom, or press the Cancel button to keep the Xoom on. Powering down the Xoom saves battery power, but know that powering up the device again is not instantaneous.

Is There a Sleep Button?

The Power/Lock button is the sleep button. Quickly pressing the Power/Lock button and releasing it turns off Xoom's screen and puts it to sleep. Another fast press and release of the button immediately turns Xoom back on.

If the Xoom is in Sleep Mode and you press the Power/Lock button to turn it back on, you also need to unlock the device before using it. Touch and hold your finger on the small padlock icon on the screen and then drag it any-where outside of the large circle that appears around the padlock icon.

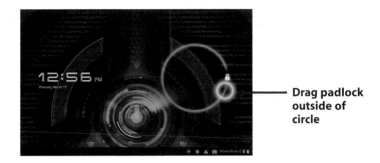

Drag padlock outside of circle

Volume Controls

On the left edge of the Xoom (while holding the device in landscape mode) toward the top of the device are two small buttons. The top button increases the volume, and the bottom button decreases it. As you increase or decrease the volume, a volume bar displays on the Xoom's screen and moves left (decrease) or right (increase) to indicate the speaker volume.

Volume Increase/ Decrease

Ports

The charging port is where you plug in the Xoom to charge the battery.

The HDMI port enables you to connect your Xoom to a larger display (such as an LCD screen) using an HDMI cable.

You use the micro USB port to connect your Xoom to other devices, such as computers or laptops. You can use the micro USB port to "mount" the device to a computer/laptop; the Xoom's files appear as a folder, and files can be moved to and from the Xoom by using standard drag-and-drop or copy/paste techniques. (The USB port is not used for charging, so do not attempt to use any kind of AC adapter to charge the Xoom via the USB port.)

The headphone jack (along the top edge of the Xoom) enables you to plug in a pair of headphones. With headphones plugged in, the Xoom's speakers are disabled, and the volume control buttons now control the volume of the headphones until they are unplugged.

The micro SD card slot holds an SD memory card with up to 32GB of extra storage space. Removing the SD card does not delete any files stored on it, but the Xoom is unable to access these files until the card is reinserted.

Cameras

Xoom comes with a 5-megapixel digital camera; the camera is mounted on the back of the Xoom (also known as rear-facing), just a short distance from the Power/Lock button. To use the camera, access an app (such as the Camera app) that's designed to use the camera. A flash is built into the Xoom for low-light environments. The camera is discussed in more detail in Chapter 6, "Photos and Video."

Xoom also includes a 2-megapixel webcam. The webcam is on the black border just above the top edge of the display screen. It can be used by any app designed to access the front-facing device. Using the webcam for video chats will be covered in Chapter 11, "Webcam, Text, and Phone Chats."

Xoom's User Interface Buttons

After turning on the Xoom and unlocking the screen, the touch screen displays a collection of icons that include a Google search bar, a Voice Actions icon, an Apps icon, a Home Screen Customization button, the Back/Home/Recent Apps button collection, the current time, and notification alerts.

Voice Actions

Apps

Home Screen Customization

Google search bar

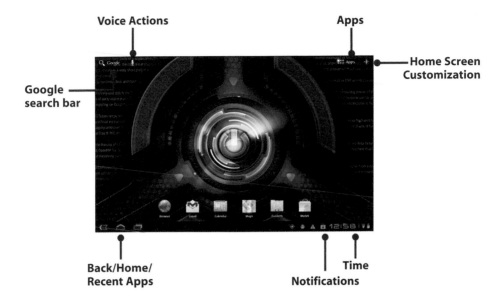

Back/Home/ Recent Apps

Time

Notifications

Google Search Bar

Tapping once on the Google search bar opens the onscreen keyboard and a text box (top-left of the screen). Enter text for your search using the keyboard, and press Return to submit the search request. A browser window opens and displays your search results.

Google search bar

Voice Actions Button

The Xoom is capable of performing searches (using Google), opening apps, sending emails, playing specific songs, providing driving directions, and more. Tap once on the Voice Actions button and speak your command when the Speak Now window appears. (Click the Help button to see examples of all the various tasks you can perform with voice actions.)

Help ────

Apps Icon

Tapping once on the Apps icon opens a window that displays all the apps installed on the Xoom. Tapping the My Apps option displays apps that you have chosen to download and install. The All option displays your personal apps and the default ones that come standard with the Xoom Android 3.0 operating system.

My Apps

All ────

Home Screen Customization Button

The Home Screen Customization button enables you to drag and drop apps and widgets, as well as change the wallpaper that displays as the screen background. A total of five home screens are available for customization, and the center screen is designated as the primary home screen. Apps, widgets, and changing wallpaper are covered in Chapter 2, "Configuring Your Xoom."

Primary home screen

Back/Home/Recent Apps Button Collection

The Back, Home, and Recent Apps buttons are in the lower-left corner of the touch screen.

When tapped, the Back button always takes you back to the screen you were previously viewing. The Home button always returns you to Xoom's primary home screen.

Tapping the Recent Apps button displays five thumbnails along the left edge of the screen that represent the last five apps you used. Tap one of the five apps to immediately jump to that selected app.

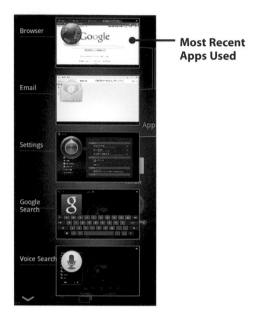

Most Recent
Apps Used

Current Time

The current time always displays in the lower-right corner of the screen. Tap
once on the time to expand the window to display day, date, time, battery
charge percentage, and other data. Tap again to expand the window to show
screen controls, such as brightness, screen lock setting, and Airplane Mode.
Tap anywhere on the screen (other than in the expanded Time window) to
close the expanded Time window.

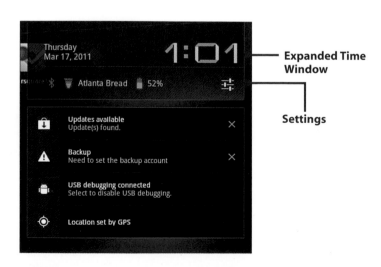

Expanded Time
Window

Settings

Notification Alerts

The Xoom can provide different types of alerts, such as calendar reminders, app installation notices, detection of Wi-Fi hotspots, and more. Notifications appear as small icons with checkmarks; tap an icon to view the alert or expand the Current Time window (refer to the previous section), and all alerts are displayed below the current time/date. You can tap the small X to the right of an alert to acknowledge the alert and remove it.

Click to close

Xoom Home Screens

When you turn on the Xoom, the screen displays a single screen, also known as a home screen. A home screen can be customized by adding and removing apps, icons, widgets, wallpaper, and more.

The Xoom provides you with five home screens. Each home screen can be uniquely customized (with the exception of wallpaper, which is shared between home screens), meaning that you could have one home screen that has your games apps, for example, and another home screen with shortcuts to your favorite websites.

Can You Add More Home Screens?
At this time, it's not possible to add more home screens. A future update to the Honeycomb operating system might allow more home screens to be created, but for now, the Xoom is locked with five.

You can view thumbnails of all five home screens by clicking the Home Screen Customization button. All five screens are displayed along the top. The center screen serves as the primary home screen, which is always displayed when the Home button is pressed.

You move from home screen to home screen by using a swipe gesture (covered in the next section).

Primary home screen

Xoom Gestures

You use touch screen devices with your fingers; tapping an icon opens it, for example. However, touch screen devices such as the Xoom are capable of interpreting more than a single tap of a finger. Most touch screen devices now come with a small collection of gestures that are shortcuts for performing actions that might otherwise require two or more taps of your finger. When using the Xoom's touch screen, the five options available are tapping, swiping, dragging, pinching, and twisting.

Tapping

This is an easy one. Touching one finger quickly on the screen is called a tap. Tapping is the most common gesture you use with the Xoom. It can open apps, place the cursor in text boxes, select menu options, and other tasks.

Dragging

Dragging is similar to tapping, but it involves placing a finger on the screen and holding it there. You can drag items, such as apps, from place to place by tapping and holding your finger on the item and moving it up, down, left, and right. Releasing your finger "drops" the item you're moving at its current location. (If an item is dropped at a location that isn't allowed, the item typically returns to its original location when you release your finger.)

Swiping

Swiping and dragging are almost identical, but swiping is more like turning a page in a book, with a fast drag followed by a quick release. It's used not so much for moving items around, but for flipping the virtual screen of the

Xoom. You use this gesture, for example, to turn the page when reading a digital book (eBook). You simply place your finger on the screen and quickly swipe it left or right, which makes the screen display a page that turns. You also perform this action to move back and forth between the five home screens that are part of the Xoom's user interface.

Pinching

Two types of pinching exist. The first involves placing two fingers (typically your thumb and pointer finger) on the screen and then moving them together. Imagine your thumb and pointer finger picking up a grain of rice.

The second type of pinching (also known as reverse-pinching) is simply a reversal of the first method. In this case, you place your touching thumb and pointer finger on the screen and then move the two fingers apart (but keeping them in contact with the screen).

These gestures are typically used to zoom in and zoom out on items such as digital photos, websites, and eBooks. A photo, for example, can be enlarged (zoomed in) by performing the reverse-pinch. This enlarges the photo. To shrink the photo, you perform the basic pinch gesture.

Twisting

The twisting gesture isn't as popular (yet) as the other four gestures, and few apps use it. Twisting involves placing two fingers (typically your left and right pointer fingers) on the screen and then moving them in opposite directions. Think of clockwise and counter-clockwise movements; moving your right pointer finger counter-clockwise and your left pointer finger clockwise causes an onscreen item to rotate counter-clockwise. The reverse gesture causes the item to rotate in a clockwise manner.

How Is the Twisting Gesture Used by the Xoom?

The twisting gesture is used in some paint/graphic design apps for rotating an object in place. Another app (covered in Chapter 8, "GPS and Navigation") that can use the twisting gesture is Google Maps. Although most maps are bird's eye views (looking straight down at streets and buildings), Google Maps allows you to use the twisting gesture to rotate the map so the view is angled and buildings and streets appear three-dimensional (also called an orthogonal view).

**Google Maps
orthogonal view**

Xoom Settings

The Xoom provides access to 12 uniquely detailed settings screens. These settings relate to how the Xoom functions, and many of them provide you with the ability to turn on and off many settings that can save battery power, shut down apps, increase security, and more.

To access Settings, tap the Apps button in the upper-right corner of the screen and tap the Settings app. You can also access Settings by tapping the current time in the lower-right corner of the screen twice (to fully expand it). Tap the Settings option at the bottom of the list.

Wireless & Networks

Use the Wireless & Networks setting screen to connect to Wi-Fi hotspots (providing login credentials such as WEP/WAP passwords, if necessary), configure Bluetooth devices (such as an external keyboard), set up the Xoom to act as a portable hotspot, enable/disable Airplane Mode (when flying), and more.

Sound

The Sound setting enables you to configure the volume of the Xoom device and adjust alert-notice volumes and alarms. An additional feature enables you to enable/disable screen-lock sounds and sound cues when selecting items on the screen (using a touch gesture).

Screen

The Screen setting controls the screen's brightness and settings related to automatic sleep time and disabling auto-rotation. Auto-rotation occurs when you rotate the Xoom; the screen changes to display either in widescreen view (the Xoom screen is wider than it is taller) or in long view (the Xoom is held vertically so the screen is taller than it is wider).

Location & Security

The Xoom can use GPS and Internet services (such as Google search) to accurately determine its location on a map. The Location & Security feature is used by many social apps (such as Foursquare or Google Locations) to provide the location of the user. Use this screen to enable/disable this feature and other security features, such as hiding passwords as they are typed and turning on a tablet PIN pad that requires a code.

Applications

The Applications setting is where you can view existing apps that are running, shut down apps, and uninstall apps. You also have access to information related to storage and battery consumption by apps.

Accounts & Sync

The Xoom is capable of synchronizing the Calendar and Contacts apps with accounts such as Google, Facebook, and more. Use this screen to enable or disable account synchronization.

Privacy

If you have created a Google user account and enable synchronization of your data, you also have the ability to back up your data from the Xoom to Google's servers (or to disable this feature). A factory reset can also be done here (resetting the Xoom by wiping all apps and user-customized settings).

Storage

In Storage, you can view the total memory storage of the Xoom device, including memory used and available. If a micro SD memory card is inserted, this screen provides the details on its storage capabilities.

Language & Input

Use the Language & Input screen to configure the language to be used and voice recognition and text-to-speech options. Keyboard settings are also customizable.

Accessibility

You enable two features, TalkBack and SoundBack, on the Accessibility screen, allowing anything you type or read (such as a web page) to be converted into a digital voice that you hear using Xoom's speakers or headphones.

Date & Time

The Date & Time setting enables you to set the date and time, as well as time zone and format (24 hours) of the time and date display.

About Tablet

You can view information on the current version of the Android operating system, as well as more detailed information, such as model number and build number (useful to software developers). You can also view details on battery usage and see what services and apps are draining the battery the most.

Configure wallpaper, desktop apps, and more using the Xoom's touch screen, and customize your Xoom to make it your own.

In this chapter, you learn how to customize your Xoom, including modifying the home screens by adding apps, changing the background wallpaper, turning on security, and setting other personalization features.

2

→ Adding an App to a Home Screen

→ Moving an App to a New Location

→ Removing an App from a Home Screen

→ Changing Your Home Screen Wallpaper

→ Adding a Widget to a Home Screen

→ Jumping to a Home Screen with No Swiping

→ Setting the Date and Time

→ Using the Lock Screen for Security

→ Changing Screen Timeout

→ Performing a Google Search

Configuring Your Xoom

The Xoom is not a device that locks you into using it in one particular manner. There are plenty of ways to make Xoom more efficient and fun.

Because the Xoom is a touch screen tablet, most of the customizations you perform require nothing more than a few gestures (taps and drags being the most common). Making changes to the Xoom's user interface is easy, and so is reversing your changes, should you find that something doesn't fit well with the way you use your tablet.

Adding an App to a Home Screen

All of your apps can be accessed by using the Apps icon in the upper-right corner of the screen. For faster access, you can also directly add shortcuts to apps to any of the five home screens.

1. Tap the Apps icon in the upper-right corner of the screen.

2. Tap and hold your finger on the app you want to add to a home screen.

3. Drag the app to one of the five home screens along bottom of the display and release your finger.

4. Drag any additional app shortcuts to any of the five home screens.

5. Tap on a home screen along the bottom of the display to immediately open that home screen.

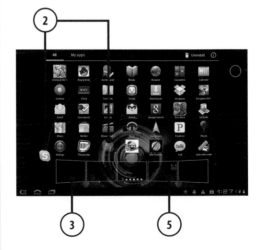

View Larger Home Screen Details

While dragging an app to a home screen, if you hold the app over a particular home screen for two seconds, that home screen enlarges to approximately 50 percent of the display, enabling you to view other app shortcuts and widgets that exist on that home screen. If you change your mind about placing an app shortcut, simply drag it out of the yellow box that represents the home screen and release your finger.

Moving an App to a New Location

Apps can easily be moved from home screen to home screen, enabling you to create customized home screens, such as a game home screen (with all gaming apps) or a social home screen (for email, messaging, Facebook, and so on).

1. Locate an app that you want to move to another home screen.

2. Tap and hold the app.

3. A line displays at the left or right edge (or both), indicating a home screen where the app can be relocated.

4. Drag the app left or right toward an edge.

5. When the app crosses the line that represents another home screen, the current home screen disappears, and the selected home screen displays.

6. Release the app if the current home screen is the desired final location.

7. Drag the app again, left or right, if another home screen location is desired.

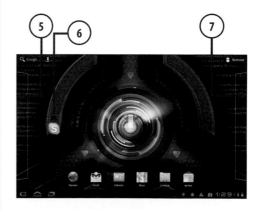

Home Screens Are Fixed Locations

Each of the five home screens has a permanent location that's relative to the other four home screens. Therefore, you cannot drag an app any further left than the leftmost home screen or any further right than the rightmost home screen. The center home screen is the default primary screen that always appears when you press the Home button.

Removing an App from a Home Screen

Removing an app from a home screen is not the same as deleting or unin-stalling the app. An app that's removed from a home screen is still available in the Apps folder, and you can access it by tapping the Apps icon in the upper-right corner of any home screen.

1. Tap and hold the app that you want to remove from a home screen.

2. The Remove icon displays in the upper-right corner of the display.

3. Drag the app to the Remove icon.

4. Lift your finger and the app is removed from the home screen.

Apps Cannot Be Moved Off-Screen

Dragging an app off-screen does not remove the app. If you attempt to drag an app icon off the screen (instead of to the Remove icon), the app drops in place at the location on the home screen closest to where you released your finger.

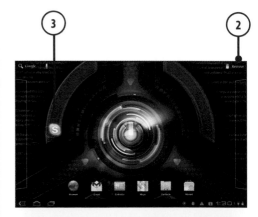

5. Tap the Apps icon.

6. Verify that the removed app is still installed by opening the Apps folder and locating the app icon.

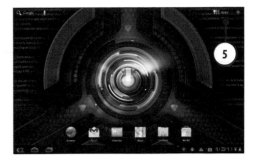

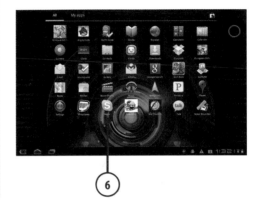

Changing Your Home Screen Wallpaper

You can easily change the default blue honeycomb wallpaper that displays on all five home screens. Possible wallpapers include static images (designs with no animation), live wallpapers (with animation), photos, and other images stored in the Gallery app.

1. Tap the Home Screen Customization button in the upper-right corner of the display.

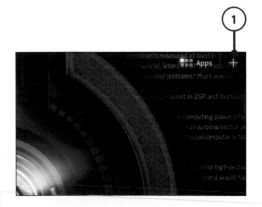

2. Tap the Wallpapers option below the five home-screen thumbnail icons.

3. Tap the Wallpapers folder to select a static (non-animated) image.

Use Your Own Photos

You can use the pictures you take with Xoom's built-in digital camera as wallpaper. To do this, select the Gallery option (instead of the Live Wallpapers or Wallpapers folders). You can find more information on taking photos and using the Gallery app in Chapter 6, "Photos and Video."

4. Tap a wallpaper design to select it.

5. Tap the Home button to view the selected wallpaper.

6. Again, tap the Home Screen Customization button.

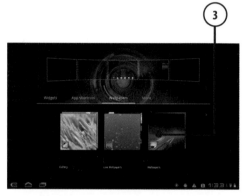

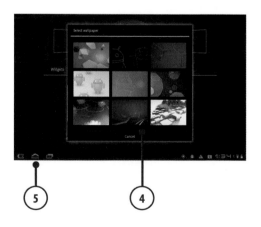

7. Tap the Live Wallpapers folder to select an animated image.

8. Tap an animated wallpaper design to select it.

9. The animated wallpaper displays on the screen.

10. Tap the Set Wallpaper button to approve the live wallpaper selection, or tap the Back button to return to the Live Wallpapers selection screen.

Animation Drains Battery Power

Animated live wallpapers are interesting and fun, but keep in mind that the animation drains the Xoom's battery more quickly. Do not choose a live wallpaper if you want to maximize your Xoom's battery life.

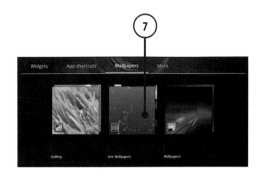

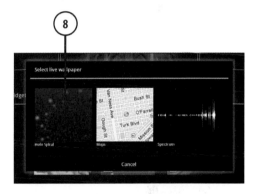

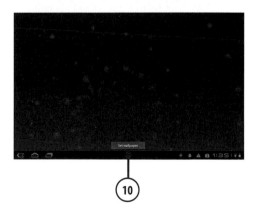

Adding a Widget to a Home Screen

Widgets are similar to apps, but they typically appear as a larger icon on a home screen and come with their own customization settings. More than a dozen widgets are included for you to try out.

1. Tap the Home Screen Customization button. (Alternatively, tap and hold anywhere on the home screen.)

2. Tap the Widgets option below the five home-screen thumbnail icons.

3. Use your finger to swipe on the Widgets display window to browse all the available widgets.

4. Tap and hold on a widget to select it.

5. Drag the widget to one of the five home-screen thumbnails at the top of the display.

6. Release your finger to drop a widget on a specific home screen.

7. Tap, hold, and drag any additional widgets to any of the five home screens.

8. Tap a home-screen thumbnail to jump to that home screen.

9. Tap a widget to use it or access its settings.

Jumping to a Home Screen Without Swiping

Because there are five home screens, it takes four different swipes of your finger to move from the farthest left home screen to the farthest right home screen. Fortunately, there's a faster way to move from home screen to home screen.

1. Tap the Home Screen Customization button (or tap and hold any blank area on a home screen).

2. Five home-screen thumbnails appear along the top of the display.

3. Tap one of the five home-screen thumbnails to immediately jump to that home screen.

Setting the Date and Time

The time always appears on the current home screen in the lower-right corner, but to view the day, date, and time, you must tap once on the time. To set the date and time, you need to access the Settings screen. (There is also a Settings link in the time widget, which appears as a three-horizontal parallel line just below the clock. Tap the Clock icon twice to see it.)

1. Tap the Apps icon in the upper-right corner of the display.

2. Tap Settings.

3. Tap Date & Time.

4. Tap Set Date.

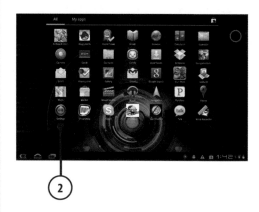

5. Use the small (up and down) triangles to select the correct month, day, and year, and then tap the Set button. (Tap Cancel to return to the Date & Time settings screen.)

6. Tap Set Time.

7. Use the small triangles to set the correct time's hours, minutes, and AM/PM setting, and then tap the Set button.

Additional Settings

You can also use the Date & Time settings screen to enable Automatic Date & Time (requires an Internet/data connection) and detect the correct time zone where the Xoom is located. Finally, you can also toggle the 24-hour format (military time) and change the date format from mm/dd/yyyy to one of three additional options.

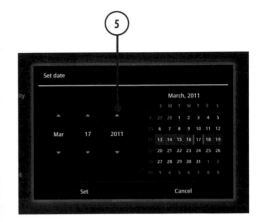

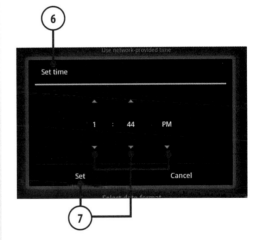

Using Lock Screen for Security

If you want to prevent someone from turning on the Xoom and accessing your apps and other information, you need to enable security. Security options include a PIN, password, or a drawn pattern.

1. Tap the Apps icon in the upper-right corner of the screen.

2. Tap Settings.

3. Tap Location & Security.

4. Tap Configure Lock Screen.

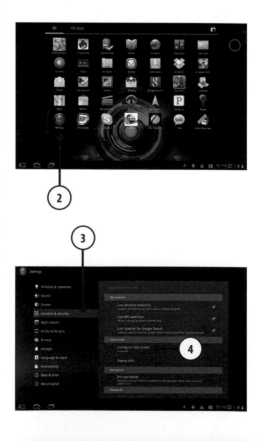

5. Tap Pattern.

6. Nine dots appear onscreen, along with instructions on how to use the Pattern option. Tap Next.

7. Use your finger to draw a pattern using the nine dots. A Pattern Recorded message appears after you lift your finger.

8. Tap the Continue button. (The Retry button enables you to draw a new pattern.)

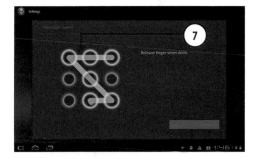

9. Use your finger to redraw the pattern and tap the Confirm button.

PIN OR PASSWORD

Although it's easy to create a complicated pattern, remembering and entering it correctly every time can become a nuisance. Instead of using a pattern, consider using the PIN (numbers) or password (text and/or numbers) options.

Also, if you ever want to disable the security feature, you are first required to enter your PIN, password, or pattern before you select the Off option that disables the lock screen feature. So, make sure that whatever option you use (PIN, password, or pattern), you can remember it and use it to unlock your Xoom.

Changing Screen Timeout

By default, the Xoom turns off the display when it detects no activity for a two-minute period. You can shorten this period (to save battery power) or lengthen it by using the Settings screen.

1. Tap the Apps icon in the upper-right corner of the screen.

2. Tap Settings.

3. Tap Screen.

4. Tap Timeout.

5. Select a timeout period of 15 seconds, 30 seconds, 1 minute, 2 minutes, 5 minutes, 10 minutes, or 30 minutes by tapping the desired time period.

Screen Brightness

The Screen selection offers you the ability to adjust the brightness of the Xoom's display. Tap Brightness and use your finger to drag the adjustment bar left (to decrease brightness) or right (to increase brightness). Remember that increasing the brightness increases battery drain.

Performing a Google Search

Rather than opening a web browser and typing www.google.com followed by your query text, Xoom keeps a Google search bar on the current home screen.

1. Tap the Google icon in the upper-left corner of the screen.

2. Use the onscreen keyboard to type your query text.

3. Tap the Enter button to begin your search, or tap one of the auto-find options listed below the Google search bar.

4. Tap the X to delete the text you typed into the search bar.

5. Results for your query text are displayed in a browser window.

6. Tap the X on the open browser window to close it.

7. Tap a query result in the open browser window; you are taken to that web page.

8. Tap the Back button to return to either the Google search bar (if you haven't tapped on a query result link) or the previous web page.

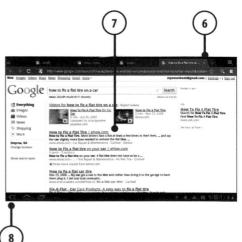

9. While the Google search bar is open, tap the Settings icon in the upper-right corner.

10. Tap Search Settings.

11. Place checks in the boxes next to the resources that you want Google to search. Options include the web, your apps, your contacts, and more.

Experimenting with Additional Settings

You probably discovered that the Settings screen has many more additional configuration options than what's covered in this chapter. Experiment with the settings to determine what works best for you.

1. Tap the Apps button in the upper-right corner of the screen.

2. Tap Settings.

3. Select one of the 12 categories listed on the left.

4. Additional configuration items appear on the right.

5. Tap an additional configuration option to view its particular capabilities.

Make One Change at a Time

Don't make a lot of settings changes at once; you can quickly forget what options you've turned on and off. Instead, make a single settings change and determine wheher you like the results. If you don't, change back to the previous setting.

Configure Wi-Fi and 3G/4G data connectivity and security settings to get your Xoom online.

Although the Xoom is designed to support data via the 3G/4G data service from your provider, the device is also capable of joining Wi-Fi networks and connecting to a laptop or computer for file transfers. The Xoom is also capable of sharing a network connection with other devices (tethering). In this chapter, you learn all about these tasks and more.

Get Connected

The Xoom offers both data (3G/4G) connectivity and Wi-Fi connectivity, which enables users to select a method for connecting to the web, checking email, downloading files, and more.

3G and 4G data service depends on your carrier, and the method for signing up and using this service differs from carrier to carrier. Consult your carrier for information related to using 3G/4G data service and any technical errors you have with that service.

Wi-Fi service, however, is identical for all Xoom devices, and the Xoom is capable of detecting 802.11a/b/c/g/n signals. Before you use Wi-Fi service, however, you must enable it.

Turning on Wi-Fi Service

Before browsing the web, sending an email, or watching an online movie, you must first turn on the Wi-Fi service (unless 3G service is enabled) for Xoom.

1. Tap the Apps icon in the upper-right corner of the screen.

2. Tap the Settings app.

3. Select the Wireless & Networks option.

4. Tap the checkbox to the right of the Wi-Fi option to place a check in the box. A Turning On message displays underneath this option.

Enabling Wi-Fi Is Different Than Joining a Wi-Fi Network

Wi-Fi must be turned on for Xoom to scan for nearby Wi-Fi networks. Even if a network is not found, the Wi-Fi service remains on, because it continually scans for a network. If you want the scanning process to stop, tap the checkbox to the right of the Wi-Fi option to remove the check and disable the service.

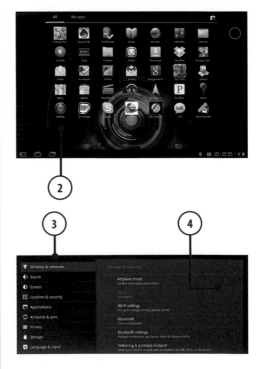

5. The Xoom starts scanning for available Wi-Fi networks to join.

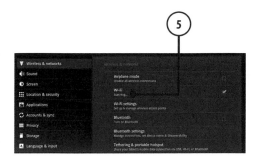

Joining a Wi-Fi Network

After Wi-Fi service is enabled, you need to configure a few settings to join a Wi-Fi network. Navigate to the Settings screen and select the Wireless & Networks option, as described in the previous section.

1. Tap the Wi-Fi Settings option.

2. View the list of available Wi-Fi networks and tap one to join it. A small padlock symbol indicates that a password is required to join.

3. Enter the password to join the Wi-Fi network. Place a check in the Show Password box if you want to see the actual password as it is being typed.

4. Tap the Connect button.

5. The Xoom attempts to obtain an IP address from the network.

6. When a connection is made, the Wi-Fi network indicates that the Xoom is connected.

Only Wi-Fi Networks That Broadcast SSID Are Visible

Each Wi-Fi network that is visible to Xoom is broadcasting its SSID (name). Some Wi-Fi networks can be configured to hide their SSID, making it more difficult to join.

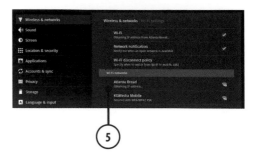

Joining a Hidden Wi-Fi Network

If the Wi-Fi network you want to join is not broadcasting its SSID (name), you can still join it if you know the SSID and password.

1. Tap the Add Wi-Fi Network option.

2. Enter the SSID of the Wi-Fi network.

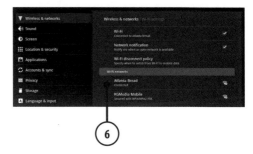

3. For Security, click the small arrow and select the type of encryption being used by the Wi-Fi network you are joining.

4. Enter the password for the Wi-Fi network.

5. If the Wi-Fi network is in range, and you provided the correct SSID and password, the Xoom connects to the network.

6. If the Wi-Fi network is out of range, the SSID and password are saved until the network is in range. Then, a connection is attempted.

Multiple Available Wi-Fi Networks

If multiple Wi-Fi networks are in range and available and you have the proper SSID and passwords saved, Xoom attempts to join them in the order they appear in the list.

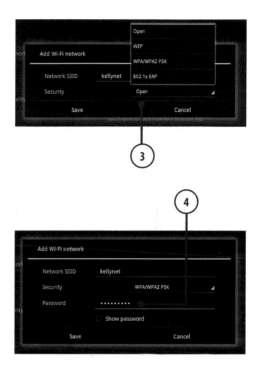

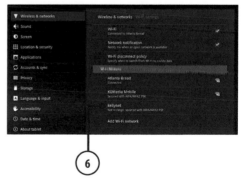

Activating Airplane Mode

The Xoom offers the capability to disable all signal communications, including text messaging and making and receiving phone calls. This is called Airplane Mode, and enabling this mode disables both 3G/4G and Wi-Fi signals.

1. Open the Settings screen and tap the Wireless & Networks option.

2. Tap the Airplane Mode option to place a check in the checkbox.

3. When the Airplane Mode checkbox is checked, Wi-Fi and 3G/4G data services are disabled. The Wi-Fi service is disabled, and the check is removed from the checkbox.

4. Tap the Airplane Mode option to remove the check from the checkbox and re-enable Wi-Fi and 3G/4G capabilities.

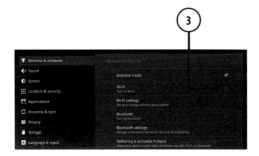

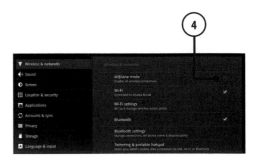

Airplane Mode Does Not Disable Bluetooth

Although Bluetooth uses a radio signal for communication, enabling Airplane Mode does not block Bluetooth; this allows users to continue using, for example, a Bluetooth headset to listen to a movie or music.

Turning on Bluetooth Service

Bluetooth service enables users to connect Bluetooth devices (such as a headset or keyboard) to the Xoom. Bluetooth devices must typically be within 15 to 30 feet (5 to 10 meters) of the device, and they often require a code (similar to a Wi-Fi password) to create a link. Before linking a Bluetooth device to the Xoom, however, you must first enable Bluetooth services.

1. On the Settings screen, tap the Wireless & Networks option, as described in the section, "Turning on Wi-Fi Service."

2. Tap once on the Bluetooth option to place a checkmark in the checkbox.

3. Tap again on the Bluetooth option to remove the checkmark and disable Bluetooth services.

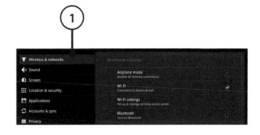

Configuring Bluetooth Service

After Bluetooth service is enabled, you can change the name being broadcast (Xoom, by default), make the Xoom discoverable to other Bluetooth devices, and find and pair (link) with Bluetooth devices.

1. On the Settings screen, tap on the Wireless & Networks option.

2. Tap the Bluetooth Settings option.

3. Tap Device Name.

4. Enter a new Bluetooth name and tap OK.

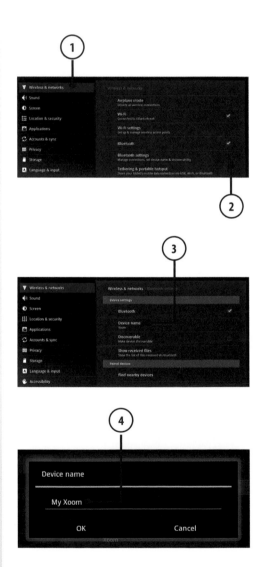

5. Tap the Discoverable option to place a checkmark in the checkbox and make the Xoom visible to other Bluetooth devices for 120 seconds.

6. Tap the Find Nearby Devices option.

7. Tap on a Bluetooth device.

8. Enter the PIN and tap the OK button to pair with it.

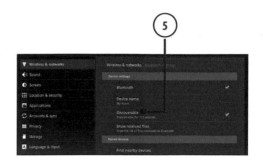

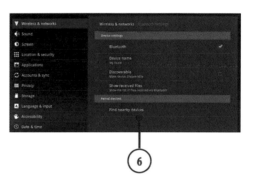

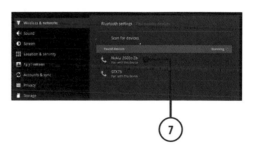

Creating a Hotspot (Tethering)

If your Xoom has 3G/4G connectivity to the Internet, you can configure the Xoom to enable other devices to access the Internet using a technique called *tethering*.

Imagine that you have your Xoom and a laptop in your car and are miles away from a Wi-Fi hotspot, but your Xoom has a 3G data signal. If you need to run an application on the laptop that uploads data to the Internet, you simply configure the Xoom to act as a Wi-Fi hotspot, turn on your laptop, join the Xoom's Wi-Fi network, and you're in business! The laptop accesses the Internet via the Xoom's 3G/4G service.

You can create the tether with a USB cable, a Wi-Fi connection, or via Bluetooth.

1. On the Settings screen, tap the Wireless & Networks option.

2. Tap the Tethering & Portable Hotspot option.

3. Place a checkmark in the USB Tethering (the cable must be connected first), Portable Wi-Fi Hotspot, or Bluetooth Tethering checkbox to create the tether.

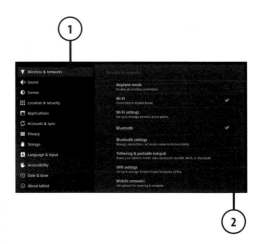

4. If the Portable Wi-Fi Hotspot is enabled, click the Portable Wi-Fi Hotspot Settings option.

5. Tap the Configure a Wi-Fi Hotspot option.

6. Create a SSID name (or use the default, AndroidAP), select either Open or WPA2 PSK for the Security option, and tap Save.

7. Devices capable of joining Wi-Fi networks need to join the new Xoom hotspot using the SSID (and a password, if required) before accessing the Internet via the Xoom's 3G/4G data service.

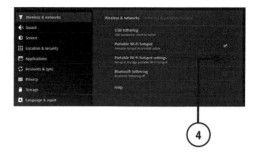

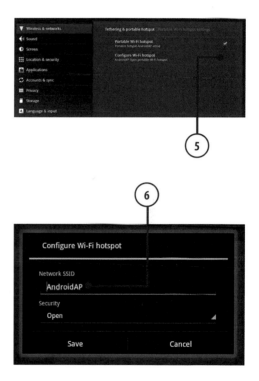

Joining a VPN

Virtual private networks (VPNs) provide a method for a device, such as the Xoom, to access a private network (such as an employer's network) using the Internet. This connection is done using encryption to securely allow information to move back and forth. Because of this, configuring your Xoom to use a VPN is more complicated than setting up a Wi-Fi network.

You need to communicate with the VPN's network administrator/IT department to obtain the correct information before you create the VPN connection with your Xoom.

1. Open the Settings screen and tap the Wireless & Networks option.

2. Tap on the VPN Settings option.

3. Tap Add VPN.

4. Select one of the four types of VPN encryption standards. (You need to get this information from the VPN network administrator/IT department.)

5. For any of the four types of VPN, you need to configure the VPN name and set a VPN server. Additional information that might be required includes keys (passwords) and Domain Name Server (DNS) information.

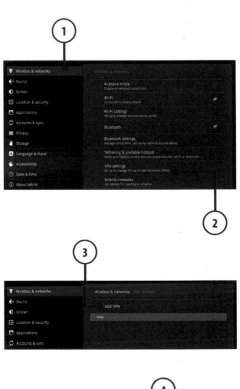

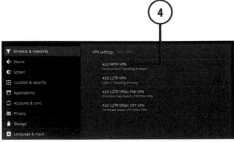

VPNs Can Be Tricky

Because VPNs primarily provide access to a private network using a non-secure Internet connection (such as from your home or a coffee shop), they often require more configuration settings than you might be used to. There are a number of methods for creating a VPN connection, and only the IT department or administrator for the VPN can provide the proper information for setting up a VPN connection between the Xoom and the private network. Do not attempt to create a VPN connection unless you have been provided with the correct information, such as a VPN name, server IP address, and password/key requirements.

Synchronizing Data

Whether you are using 3G/4G data service or a Wi-Fi connection, your Xoom is capable of synchronizing information such as your contacts (email, phone numbers, addresses, and more) and calendar with the built-in Contacts and Calendar apps. If you're using a Google user account, additional information that can be synced includes your actual Gmail (Google email) and any books that you purchased from the Google Bookstore.

Using this feature (and others, such as Google Docs or Google Calendar, which are covered in other chapters) requires that you have a user account set up, such as a Google user account. (You should have already created a free Google account when you first powered up the Xoom, but if you chose to skip that step, you can add one now.)

1. On the Settings screen, tap the Accounts & Sync option.

2. Click the Add Account link in the upper-right corner of the screen.

3. Select Corporate, Email, Google, or Skype and follow the instructions to add that account to the Xoom. (For the remaining examples, I use a Google account to demonstrate data synchronization.)

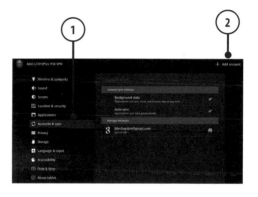

What Is Synchronization?

The Xoom can be configured to maintain a copy of your Google email, contact information, calendar, and more on the device, even if data service is interrupted. By synchronizing your Google contacts, for example, you have access to a friend's phone number and address even if your Wi-Fi or 3G data service isn't working. Synchronization typically works in both directions; if you update a friend's email address or add a reminder to the Xoom Calendar app, this information is copied back (synced) to the user's contacts or calendar.

4. Tap the user account you added.

5. Tap individual checkboxes to enable or disable the synchronization of various types of data with your Xoom.

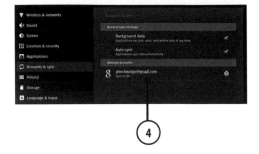

6. Below each type of data, you see a date and time that represents when that data was last synced with the Xoom. To immediately sync the data, tap the item to remove the checkmark and then tap again to add the checkmark.

7. Data being synchronized has a small sync icon next to the checkmark.

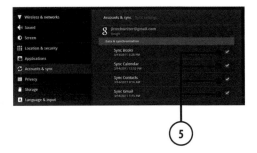

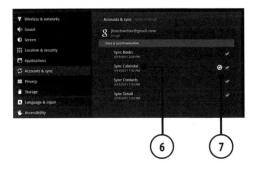

It's Not All Good

SYNCHRONIZATION REQUIRES A DATA CONNECTION

Keep in mind that synchronizing user account data with the Xoom requires either a 3G/4G data or Wi-Fi connection. Any data that has changed with the user account (such as a contact's email address or an appointment set by an assistant in your calendar) after the last synchronization does not show up on the Xoom until you perform a data sync.

Connecting to a Windows Laptop or Computer

Using the Xoom's USB cable (although any Type A to Micro B cable works), you can connect the Xoom to your Windows PC or laptop and easily move files back and forth. The Xoom presents itself as a storage device and provides you with access to its folders.

1. Connect your Xoom to your computer or laptop.

2. Click the Start button on your computer or laptop, and select Computer (or My Computer).

CONNECTING TO DIFFERENT OPERATING SYSTEMS

Go Further >>>

The procedure for connecting the Xoom is slightly different for different operating systems (OSs), so be sure to read all onscreen prompts that appear when you first connect the Xoom via USB cable.

For some OSs (especially Windows XP and Windows Vista), you might be asked to provide a device driver for the Xoom. You can find the correct Xoom driver for your OS by visiting www.motorola.com/Support/US-EN/Support-Homepage/Software_and_Drivers/USB-and-PC-Charging-Drivers.

3. When the computer window opens, double-click the Xoom icon.

4. Open and expand the Device Storage option to view the Xoom's folder structure.

5. Drag and drop or copy and paste files and folders in between Windows and the Xoom folders as needed. (Avoid any of the other folders as they typically contain system files related to Android working properly. Tinkering in these folders could crash your Xoom.)

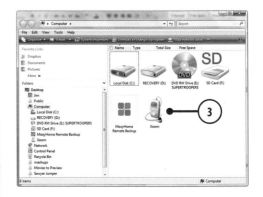

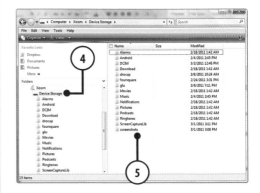

Music, Movies, and Other File Types

You can easily copy MP3 music files, videos (such as mpeg or AVI), and other file types back and forth between your computer and your Xoom. The Xoom comes with a Download folder, which is great for storing files (and finding them), but you can also use the Music, Movies, or Pictures folders. Using the proper folder (the Pictures folder for JPEGs, for example) ensures that the file is available when you use the proper app, such as Gallery (for photos) and Music (for, well, music).

With an Internet connection and a browser app for your Xoom, the Internet is wide open with video, blogs, games, and more.

With the Xoom's large display, surfing the web won't give you headaches from squinting your eyes at the screen. The Xoom has many features and capabilities, but one of the most enjoyable is using a simple web browser to explore sites of interest, all from a comfortable chair... or any location you choose.

Browsing the Web

Xoom comes with a standard web browser app called...Browser. You're certainly not locked into using it, and you can find alternative web browsers available in the Android Market, but it is a stable app with some great features.

The Browser app takes advantage of the Xoom's ability to display websites in either vertical or horizontal view; you simply rotate the Xoom and the display rotates and adjusts the text and images to try and fit it all on the screen. That said, you'll likely find that the horizontal view makes the fewest changes to the layout of the web pages you visit, and you only need a simple flick of the finger to have the web page scroll up or down.

All the examples in this chapter are displayed using the Browser app in horizontal view, except where specified.

Visiting a Web Page

The most basic service a web browser can provide to a user is the ability to display a web page. The Browser app does a great job of displaying websites, but be aware that, if you're using a different browser, the screenshots in this chapter might look slightly different.

1. Tap the Apps icon in the upper-right corner of the screen.

2. Tap the Browser app.

3. Tap once in the URL text field to highlight the current website's URL. The highlighted text changes to white on a green background.

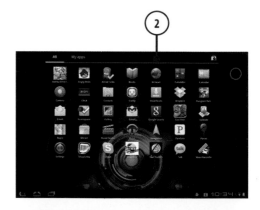

What's a URL?

What most people refer to as a web address actually has the fancy technical name: Universal Resource Locator (URL). Throughout this book, the terms *web address* and *URL* are used interchangeably and mean the same thing for all intents and purposes. If one of your techy friends emails you and says something like, "I'm including the URL at the end of this message," she's simply telling you that she's including the web address.

4. Type in a new web address using the onscreen keyboard. In this example, I typed www.quepublishing.com. (Note that the onscreen keyboard has a .com key that can save you some typing.)

5. Tap the Return/Enter key.

6. If the web address is typed correctly (and the website actually exists), the Browser app displays the website.

7. Scroll up and down the page by touching and holding your finger to the display and moving it up (to scroll up) or down (to scroll toward the bottom of the web page).

8. Typing in the website incorrectly (or entering a URL that doesn't exist) typically results in a screen letting you know that the website is unavailable. Check the URL and re-enter it if you want to try again.

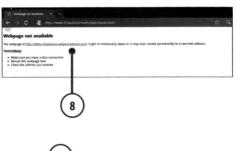

9. To close a web page, tap the small X. (If you are currently only viewing one website, this typically closes the Browser app. Viewing multiple websites is done using tabs, which is covered later.)

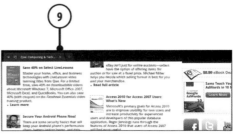

Make Your Web Browser App Easy to Find

You can always access your web browser app from the Apps folder, but if you use it frequently, consider adding a shortcut to the app on one of your five home screens. Refer to Chapter 2, "Configuring Your Xoom" for instructions on adding an app shortcut to one of your home screens.

Setting Your Homepage

The Xoom's Browser app always saves the last website you viewed unless you close it (see the previous section). Opening your web browser app again causes it to display a default webpage called a homepage. You can easily change the homepage to any website that you prefer.

1. Open the Browser app. (My home-page is set to www.google.com.)

2. Tap the menu button in the upper-right corner of the screen.

3. From the drop-down menu that appears, select Settings.

4. Select General.

5. Tap the Set Homepage option.

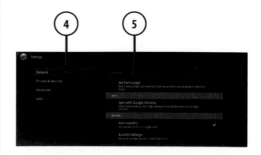

6. Use the onscreen keyboard to enter the URL of the website you want to set as your homepage, or click the Current Page button to make the currently displayed website your homepage. (I entered www.jamesfloydkelly.com.)

7. Tap OK to set the homepage to the new URL.

8. Close the current website(s) and restart the Browser app.

9. Your new homepage now appears.

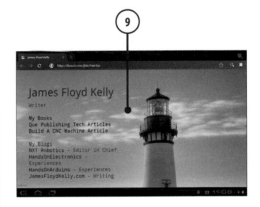

Not Every Web Browser Saves the Last-Visited Website

The Browser app saves any current websites you are viewing as long as you do not close them by clicking the X on the tab for that website. If you tap the Home button and run additional apps and then later return to the Browser app, all the websites you were viewing are remembered and displayed for you. Keep in mind, however, that this behavior might not exist in other web browsers. Also keep in mind that using the Home button often to leave apps (which keeps them running in the background) can cause memory issues, so always try to exit an app properly if you're done with it.

Creating a Bookmark

If you find yourself visiting certain websites frequently, you can save yourself some typing by adding them as bookmarks that appear in a list of favorite websites.

1. Visit a website that you frequent. In this example, I visit www.engadget.com.

2. Tap the Bookmark icon.

3. Tap the Add Bookmark option in the upper-right corner of the display.

4. The current webpage you are viewing is automatically entered.

5. Tap the Label (in this example, it's Engadget) to change it.

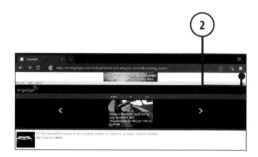

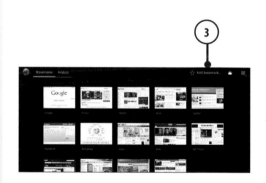

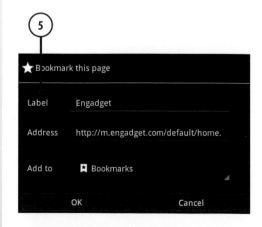

6. Enter a more descriptive label, if you desire.

7. Tap the small arrow to create another bookmark folder. (This is useful for organizing your bookmarks into categories.)

8. Tap the Other Folder option.

9. Tap the New Folder button.

10. Type in a new folder name; in this example, I create a Technology Blogs folder.

11. Click the OK button twice.

12. Your new folder appears in the Add To section.

13. Tap the OK button to save the bookmark.

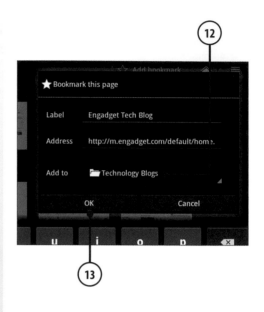

Create Additional Bookmark Folders

If you tend to frequently use bookmarks, you will want to create additional bookmark folders to organize all of your favorite sites. After you create additional folders, you can select a folder to add a bookmark by tapping the Add To button and selecting a folder from the drop-down list that appears.

Viewing Your Bookmarks

After you open the Browser app, you can easily view your bookmarks and save yourself some typing by selecting the website you want to visit with a single tap of your finger.

1. Open the Browser app and tap the Bookmarks button.

2. Tap a website thumbnail to open and view that web page.

3. Tap on a bookmark folder to open that folder and view any bookmarks saved inside.

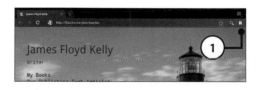

4. If you are viewing bookmarks inside a bookmark folder, tap the Back button to return to the previous page and any additional bookmark folders.

5. To delete a bookmark, tap and hold a website thumbnail.

6. From the menu window, tap the Delete Bookmark option to remove a bookmark.

7. Tap Edit Bookmark to change the bookmark's name or URL.

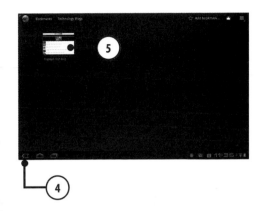

Additional Options for Bookmarks

After tapping and holding a website thumbnail, additional options available to you include the ability to add a shortcut to a home screen, share a link (via Gmail, for example), and even set the bookmarked website as the homepage.

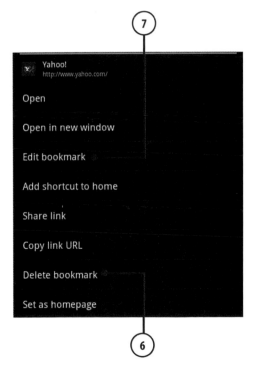

Visiting a Website in a New Tab

You don't have to close a current website you're viewing to open a new one. The Browser app enables you to simultaneously open multiple websites; with a single tap of your finger, you can jump back and forth between open websites.

1. While viewing a website, tap the + mark.

2. A new tab opens, displaying the default homepage.

3. Tap the URL text field to type in a new web address and view that website in the newly opened tab.

4. Tap the Bookmarks button to select and view a bookmarked website in the new tab.

5. Tap the + mark to open another tab.

6. Tap an existing tab to jump to that website.

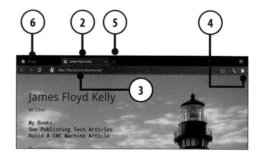

Sharing a Website

Sometimes you discover a website that you just have to share with a friend, family member, or co-worker. The Browser app lets you share the URL without having to leave the page you're viewing.

1. While viewing the webpage you want to share, tap the Menu button.

2. Tap Share Page.

3. Select Gmail (or Email if you have it configured).

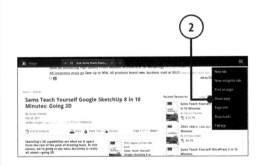

Additional Options for Bookmarks

The list of available methods for sharing a URL might be different on your Xoom because it depends on the apps that you have installed and configured. Apps that are capable of sharing text appear in the list that appears after clicking the Share button. Although email is the most frequent method for sharing URLs, the Bluetooth option can send the URL to a mobile phone, and the Dropbox option (if you have an account) saves the URL as a text file that can be accessed using the Dropbox service.

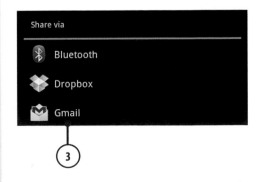

4. Enter the email address of the recipient.

5. Tap the Send button.

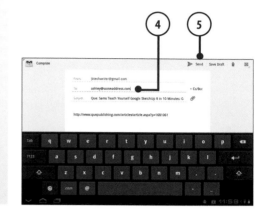

Using Favorites Homepage

The Browser app tracks the websites that you frequent the most. Instead of setting a homepage, you can configure your Xoom to display thumbnail icons of your most frequented websites when you open the Browser app.

1. Open the Browser app, tap the Menu button, and select Settings.

2. Tap Labs.

3. Tap Most Visited Homepage to place a checkmark in the checkbox.

4. Tap the Back button and close any open websites.

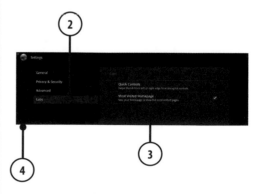

5. Open the Browser app.

6. Tap a website thumbnail to open and view that website.

6

Selecting a Default Search Engine

Xoom is set to use the Google search engine whenever you perform a search, but you can change the default search engine to Bing or Yahoo!.

1. Open the Browser app, tap the Menu button, and select Settings.

2. Tap Advanced.

3. Tap the Set Search Engine option.

4. Select Bing, Yahoo!, or Google, or click the Cancel button to keep the currently selected search engine.

1

2   **3**

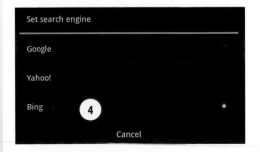

4

5. In the Browser app, tap the Search button.

6. Type the text of your search.

7. Tap the Enter key.

8. Search results are displayed using the search engine you specified.

9. Tap a link to open and view that search result.

Google Search Is Always Available

Even if you change the default search engine to Yahoo! or Bing, the Google search engine is always available on your home screens in the upper-left corner of the screen.

Using AutoFill Information

If you frequently visit websites that ask for information such as your email, street address, and ZIP code, you might like the AutoFill feature. The Browser app attempts to identify those text fields and fills them in with the information you provide. This is handy for e-commerce sites where you have to enter shipping information; the AutoFill feature does not save credit card numbers, Social Security numbers, and similar information.

1. Open the Browser app, tap the Menu button, and select Settings.

2. Select General.

3. Tap Form AutoFill if you want to disable the service; the checkmark is removed from the checkbox.

4. Tap AutoFill Settings.

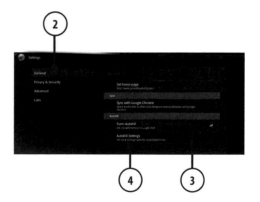

>>> Go Further

SAVED DATA CAN BE A SECURITY RISK

Although AutoFill is useful and saves time, it's also a slight security risk, because it provides anyone with access to your Xoom with information such as your address, email, and phone number. If your Xoom is not password protected and falls into the wrong hands, any data you provided to the AutoFill feature is visible. Consider using a password, PIN, or pattern (refer to Chapter 2) if you choose to use the AutoFill feature.

5. Tap in the Full Name text field and use the onscreen keyboard to enter your name.

6. Tap additional text fields to supply more information.

7. Tap Save Profile to save your AutoFill information.

8. Tap Delete Profile to delete your AutoFill information.

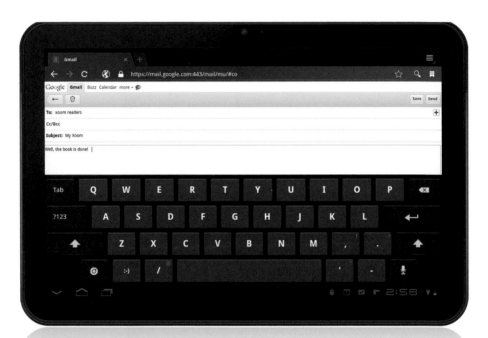

Email support is available on your Xoom for every user— Gmail, Hotmail, Yahoo!, Exchange, and more.

In addition to surfing the web, the Xoom
handles email with style. Not only does it
come with a built-in app for Gmail but you
also have the option to configure the Email
app for any other email addresses you
have—Yahoo!, Hotmail, and even a work or
personal email address from your own
registered domain.

5

Using Email

Xoom comes standard with both the Gmail app and the Email
app. There are plenty of other email apps available in the
Android Market (see Chapter 7, "The Android Market," for more
information on the Android Market), but the Gmail and Email
apps are fairly easy to configure and use, and you might find
that they're all you need to take care of your email needs.

The Gmail app is for Google email addresses only; you are only
able to configure this app to access email that has a corre-
sponding Google user account. Although the Email app can
also access Gmail messages, it's more suitable for non-Gmail
email addresses, such as Hotmail, corporate, and other email
accounts. (Yahoo! users can find a special Yahoo!-specific app
available from the Android Market.)

Creating a Gmail Account

If you have not yet configured a Gmail address for use with your Xoom, the process is fast and simple. (Later in this chapter, you see how to add a different email address for use with the Email app.)

1. Tap the Apps button in the upper-right corner of the screen.

2. Tap the Gmail app.

3. The Settings screen opens. Tap the Accounts & Sync option.

4. Tap the Add Account button in the upper-right corner.

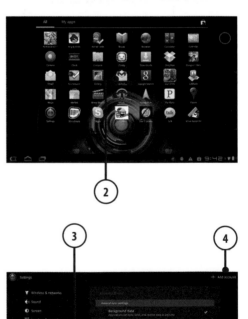

Types of Accounts

The Corporate account enables you to access a Microsoft Exchange work email address with your Xoom. You can use the Email selection for most all other types of email addresses, including Hotmail, Yahoo!, and other email services. The Skype account isn't for email, but because Skype maintains a contact database that can be synched to Xoom (see Chapter 3, "Get Connected"), it's listed as an account type that you can create.

5. Select one of the four options. For this example, select the Google option to create a Gmail address.

6. If you already have a Google user account (and Gmail address), simply enter the Gmail address and your password and click the Sign In button. The Gmail app is configured to use the existing user account and give you access to that account's Gmail.

7. To create a new Google user account, tap the Create Account button.

8. Provide your name, your login name (this is also the name portion of your @gmail.com address), a password, and the remaining requested information.

9. Scroll down the page and click the I Accept. Create My Account. button.

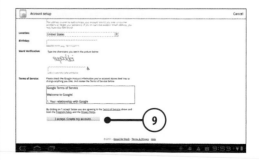

10. Enter your mobile phone number. Google needs to verify that you are creating a legitimate account (and that you're not a spammer), so Google sends you a text message or an automated phone call that provides you with a verification code.

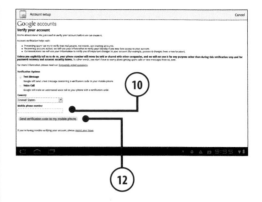

11. Select your verification option.

12. Click the Send Verification Code to My Mobile Phone button.

13. Enter the verification code you received via text or automated phone message.

14. Tap the Verify button.

15. Your account is created. You can view it using the Gmail app.

16. Tap the Home button to exit.

Accessing the Gmail App

Now that you have a Google user account (and matching Gmail address), you can access your Gmail with the Gmail app. It's best to use the Gmail app in horizontal mode for maximum viewing space. For the remainder of this chapter, I use Xoom in horizontal mode for all email tasks.

1. Open the Apps folder and tap the Gmail app to open it.

2. Your Gmail messages are organized in different folders with names such as Inbox, Drafts, Spam, Trash, and others.

3. Tap the Inbox to view current and new messages.

4. Tap an email on the right to open that message. Messages in bold are new and unread.

5. After you tap an email message, the text of the message appears on the right side of the screen.

6. Folders disappear on the left and are replaced with a scrolling list of new and current emails.

7. Tap the Forward button to send a copy of the email to additional recipients.

8. Tap the Reply button to respond to the sender.

9. Tap the Reply to All button to respond to all recipients (including the original sender).

10. If a photo or image is embedded in the email, tap the Show Pictures button to view any graphics.

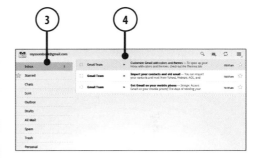

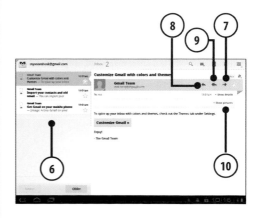

11. Tap the Back button to return to the list of Gmail folders.

12. Tap the trashcan icon to delete the message. It is moved to the Trash folder and permanently deleted after 30 days.

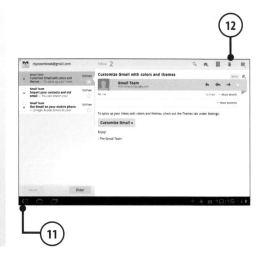

GMAIL SECURITY

Gmail accounts are not immune to hijacking—if you don't have a strong password created for your Google user account, hackers might easily crack it and take over your Gmail account, using it to send spam or other nefarious tasks. Google also isn't immune to technology problems, and it's not unheard of for some Gmail users to log in to find all of their email missing. It's rare, but it has happened. Create a strong password for your Google account and, if your email is valuable to you, consider a Gmail backup service. You can find numerous articles on how to back up your Gmail with a quick Google search for "Gmail backup."

>>> Go Further

Sending a Message with Gmail

Gmail has many features, but the most common task for most users is simply sending an email message.

1. From the folders view, tap the Compose button. (This button is also available when you open and are reading an email.)

2. Enter an email address in the To field.

3. Tap in the Subject text field to enter a subject for your message.

4. Tap in the Compose Mail area to enter your email's main message.

5. Tap the +CC/BCC button to provide additional email addresses using the CC or BCC feature.

6. Tap the Paperclip icon to add an attachment to the message.

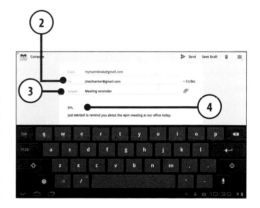

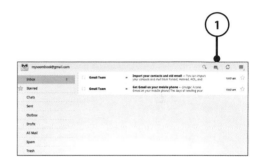

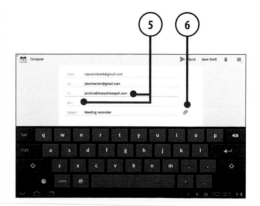

7. Browse the Camera, Download, and Screenshots folders (by tapping them to select and using the Back button to return to previous screens) and select a file.

8. Your file attachment is added to the message.

9. Tap the Send button to send the email.

Save Draft Messages and View Sent Messages

If you'd rather save a message as a draft, tap the Save Draft button instead of the Send button after composing the email. If you want to view any emails that you've sent, tap the Sent folder and tap any of the messages on the right side of the screen to open and view them.

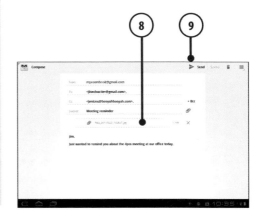

Adding a Gmail Signature

Many email users like to append a signature to the end of their messages; this signature can include things such as phone numbers, job title, contact information, and more. Many law and accounting offices are also required to include legal disclaimers. Fortunately, the Gmail app enables you to easily add one or more lines to the end of each sent email.

1. When viewing your Gmail folders, tap on the Menu icon in the upper-right corner of the screen.

2. Tap Settings.

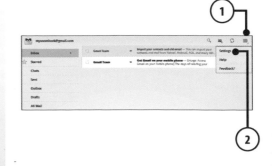

3. Tap your Gmail address to select it.

4. On the right side of the screen, tap the Signature option.

5. Enter text for your signature line.

6. Use the Enter button to start a new line of text.

7. Tap the OK button to save your new signature.

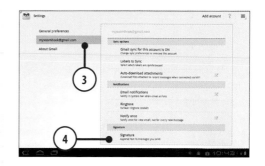

Additional Options for Your Gmail Account

In addition to adding a signature, the Settings screen for your Gmail account also enables you to turn synchronization on and off (see Chapter 3 for more information), set a tone to alert you when a message arrives, and disable alerts. Feel free to experiment with these and other settings to customize your Gmail app experience.

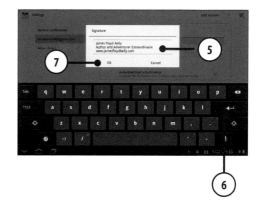

Other Gmail Options

Gmail has many more available features, and more are constantly being added.

1. Open the Gmail app, tap the Menu button, and select Settings.

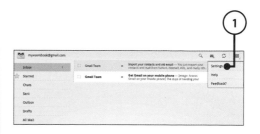

2. Tap General Preferences.

3. Tap Confirm Before Deleting to place a checkmark in the checkbox. Deleting an email opens a confirmation window for you to confirm the deletion.

4. Tap Confirm Before Sending to place a checkmark in the checkbox. Before sending a message, a pop-up window asks you to confirm the send task.

5. Tap Message Text Size to select from a list of font sizes that can increase or decrease the size of the text displayed when you open an email.

6. From within an email message, tap the Menu button.

7. Tap Mark Unread and the current message you are viewing is bolded in the Inbox.

8. Tap Report Spam and the message is moved to the Spam folder and Google is alerted.

9. Tap Help to open a web browser and view Google's Gmail Help screen; you can search for keywords or type in your question and view possible solutions/answers. For example, Gmail offers labels (instead of folders) that are extremely useful for sorting and finding email messages; the use of labels is a complex subject and is a perfect one to research with the Help screen.

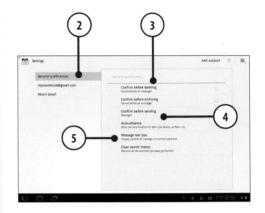

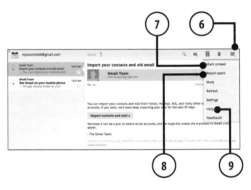

Gmail Features Galore

Some of Gmail's features, such as labels, easily require their own chapter. I encourage you to consult the Gmail Help feature to learn about all the features that are available to Gmail users.

Using the Full-Featured Browser Version of Gmail

If you're a Gmail user who prefers the complete version of Gmail that is typically seen in a browser window, you'll be pleased to know that you can bypass using the Gmail app and just use the browser-based version of Gmail.

1. Open the Browser app and enter www.gmail.com in the URL field.

2. Your Gmail messages are displayed using the Mobile format.

3. Scroll to the bottom of the window.

4. Tap the Desktop link.

Gmail for Power Users

The Gmail app is useful, but if you're a Gmail power user like me, you want to always access Gmail using the desktop browser mode. First, add your Gmail web page as a bookmark (refer to Chapter 4, "Browsing the Web"). Next, from a home screen, tap the Home Screen Customization button in the upper-right corner of the screen, tap More, tap the Bookmark icon, and select the Gmail web page you just bookmarked. Now, you can access the full-featured Gmail web page with a single tap of the shortcut icon.

5. Gmail is displayed in its general browser layout.

Configuring the Email App

If you want to access a standard email address other than a Gmail address on your Xoom, you need to use the Email app. (Microsoft Exchange email accounts require more steps—see the next section for details.)

1. Open the Apps folder and click the Email app.

2. Enter the email address and the password.

3. Tap the Next button.

4. **Tap** the Manual Setup button if you need to configure a Microsoft Exchange Server email address.

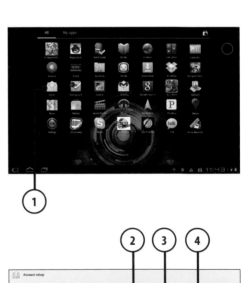

Microsoft Exchange Server and Email

If you have an email address that is supported by a Microsoft Exchange Server, you need to provide some additional information before you continue. Contact your company's IT department or email administrator for assistance, because you need to properly configure your Xoom for secure access to your email.

5. Configure any special options offered. Tap an item to remove the checkmark from the checkbox.

6. Tap the Next button to continue.

7. Provide the account with a descriptive name (optional).

8. Tap the Next button to open the Email app.

9. Tap on a folder to view its contents.

10. Email messages are displayed on the right; bold messages indicate new, unread emails.

11. Tap the Refresh button to check for new emails.

12. Tap the New Message button to compose a new email.

13. Tap the Menu button to edit account settings.

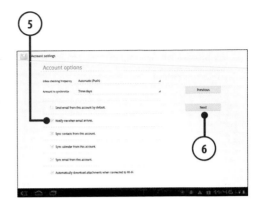

Similarities with Gmail and Email Apps

You probably noticed that the Gmail app and the Email app share a similar layout. Because of that, you might find moving from one app to the other fairly simple. The features available in each app are also similar, so if you find you need more advanced features, you either need to use the native email environment (refer to the "Using the Full-Featured Browser Version of Gmail" section), or use the Android Market to find and download a more advanced email app that can serve your needs.

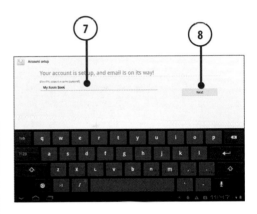

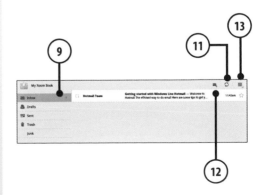

Use the built-in 5-megapixel camera to shoot photos and video that can easily be played, emailed, uploaded, and edited…all on the Xoom tablet.

In this chapter, you learn how to take digital photos and videos with the Xoom and view and share them.

Photos and Video

Your Xoom comes equipped with two cameras: a webcam and a digital camera. The webcam is used for video conferencing, and the digital camera can switch between taking photographs and shooting video.

In addition to the cameras, the Xoom also comes with two apps for viewing your photos and videos. The two apps are easy to use and, combined with a 3G/4G or Wi-Fi data connection, they make sharing your digital photos and videos extremely simple.

Taking a Digital Photo

Taking digital photos with the Xoom requires the use of the Camera app. You can find this app in the Apps folder, but you can easily create a shortcut icon on a home screen to make it easier and faster to access, which is what I did in this chapter. (See Chapter 2, "Configuring Your Xoom," for instructions on dragging an app to a home screen.)

1. Open the Camera app by tapping its icon.

2. Hold the Xoom so that the rear-facing camera is pointed toward the person or thing you want to photograph.

3. The Xoom's display shows you what the photo should look like; move the Xoom to adjust the image on the display.

4. Tap the Shutter button to take the photo.

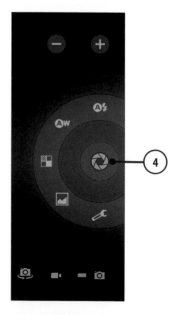

5. Tap the image thumbnail in the lower-left corner to view the most recently taken photo.

6. The most recent photo appears on the screen.

7. Tap anywhere on the screen, and a series of buttons appear along the top-right edge of the screen.

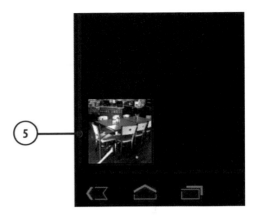

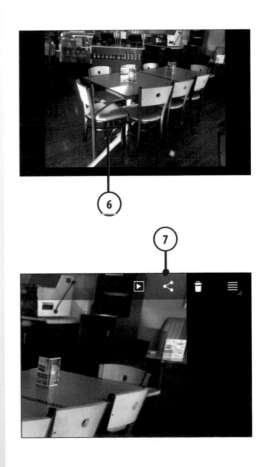

8. Tap the garbage can icon to delete the photo.

9. Tap the Share button to select a variety of services, such as Flickr or email, from a drop-down list. (Read more about sharing photos later in this chapter.)

10. Tap the Slideshow button to have the Xoom cycle through all photos stored in the Gallery app, starting from the most recent to the oldest.

11. Tap the Menu button to see more options for manipulating your photo.

12. Tap Rotate Left or Rotate Right to rotate the photo 90 degrees.

13. Tap Set Picture As to assign the image to a contact or to make it the Xoom's wallpaper.

14. Tap the Details button to view information such as the photo size (in megabytes), the time the photo was taken, and camera settings.

15. Tap the Crop button.

16. A blue box appears on the photo, representing where the crop (cut) will be made.

17. Tap and hold the right edge of the box and drag it to the right; you see the <> symbols appear on the line as you drag it.

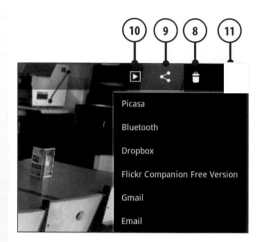

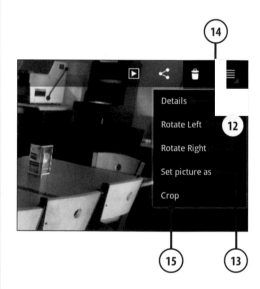

18. Tap and hold the top edge, bottom edge, and left edge, and drag these edges until you are satisfied with the crop area.

19. Tap the OK button to save the crop as a separate image. (The original is left in the Gallery, unchanged.)

20. The photo is cropped, and the final image is displayed.

Crop Edits Create a New Photo
Cropping a photo does not delete the original. After you click the OK button to save any crop edits you make, the new image is saved as a new photo in the Gallery app, which is covered later in this chapter.

Adjusting Camera Settings

The Xoom's digital camera has many adjustable settings. For example, you can zoom in and out and turn on and off the flash.

1. While the Camera app is open, tap the Zoom In (+) button or the Zoom Out (-) button to adjust the camera's zoom.

2. Tap the Flash Mode button.

3. Select Auto, On, or Off from the pop-up menu.

4. Tap the White Balance button.

5. Select Auto, Incandescent, Daylight, or Fluorescent.

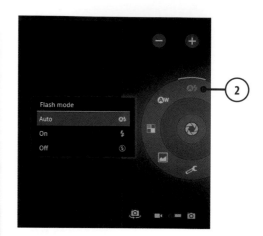

Changed Camera Settings

Changing camera settings does not affect any photos you have taken previously. Only new photos have your changes applied. Keep in mind that your setting changes are saved, and be sure to change them back if you modify a setting for a special photo.

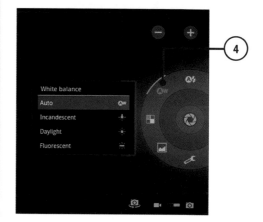

6. Tap the Color Effect button.

7. Select None, Mono, Sepia, Negative, Solarize, or Posterize.

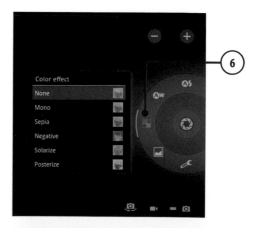

8. Tap the Scene Mode button.

9. Select one of the 12 options; each slightly tweaks Xoom's digital camera settings to achieve the best results for the selected location or conditions.

10. Tap the Camera Settings button.

11. Tap the left and right arrows to toggle on and off settings, such as Auto Focus and Store Location (GPS information tagged to a photo).

12. Other toggles allow you to specify picture size (in megapixels) and quality.

13. Tap Restore Defaults to return Xoom's digital camera to its original settings.

Taking Photos Can Be Tricky

This chapter is not meant to teach you the finer aspects of taking photos and adjusting settings, such as exposure, white balance, and focus. If you need more information on camera settings, point the Browser app to your favorite search engine and research camera settings and good photo taking.

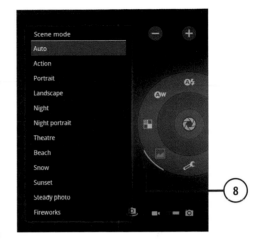

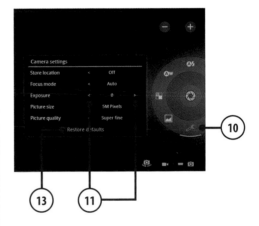

Shooting a Digital Video

In addition to taking photos, Xoom's digital camera can shoot some great video. You use the Camera app to shoot video.

1. Open the Camera app and tap the Photo/Video toggle button.

2. The Camera Toggle button switches between the digital camera on back and the webcam on front (more on this later).

3. Hold the Xoom so that the digital camera points toward your subject.

4. Tap the Record button once to start recording.

5. The length of the video is displayed as it records.

6. Tap the Record button again to stop recording.

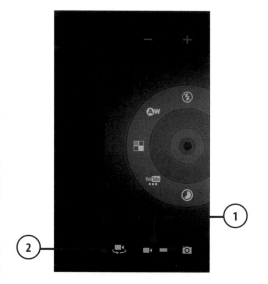

7. Tap the video thumbnail that represents the most recent video.

8. The video appears on the display.

9. Tap the Play button to watch the video.

10. Tap the garbage can icon to delete the video.

11. Tap the Share button to select a method to share the video—if the video is too large, email is not a good option. Read more about sharing videos in the section, "Sharing a Digital Photo or Video via Gmail." (The list of available methods for sharing varies depending on the apps you have installed on your Xoom.)

12. Tap the slideshow button; the first frame of any video shows up in the slideshow along with photos you took in Camera mode.

13. Tap the Menu button to view details about your video, including the time it was shot, its duration, and file size (in megabytes).

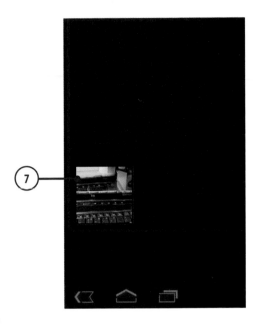

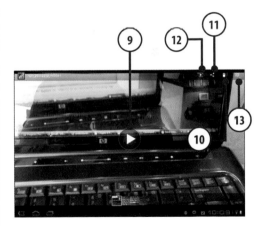

>>> *Go Further*

SHOOTING VIDEO OF YOURSELF

Because the digital camera is mounted on the back of the Xoom, it's a bit hard to shoot video of yourself (unless you have someone else to hold the Xoom or are going to hold it yourself, which results in a shaky video). A nice feature with the Camera app is the capability to select the webcam at the top of the Xoom's display to use for taking video. I cover using this in Chapter 11, "Webcam, Text, and Phone Chats," but just know that with the webcam, the video quality isn't as high as with the digital camera.

Adjusting Video Settings

The Camera app has a few settings that you can tweak for shooting video. Be aware that any changes you make to the video settings do not affect the camera settings; if you change the White Balance setting while in Video mode, for example, the same change does not occur for Camera mode should you switch and decide to take a photo.

1. While in Video mode, the Zoom In and Zoom Out buttons are disabled.

2. Tap the Flash Mode button to turn the flash on and off. In Video mode, the flash constantly stays on to act as a light in low-light settings.

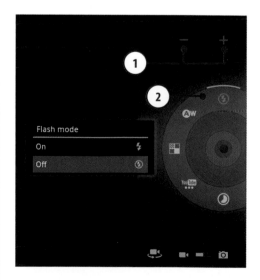

3. Tap the White Balance button to make adjustments.

4. Tap the Color Effect button to make a selection.

5. Tap the Video Quality button; High records in widescreen format, and Low records in 4:3 Standard format. Select YouTube (High, 15m) if you intend to upload the video to YouTube.

6. Tap the Time Lapse Interval button to record a video that shoots a single frame and then pauses for the selected time before shooting another frame. Options include Off (the default setting) and intervals from 1 second to 10 seconds.

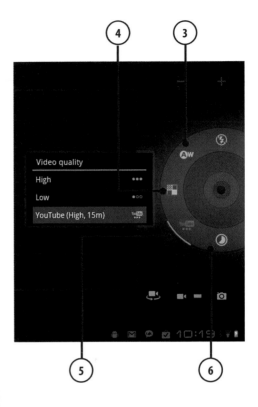

Fun with Time Lapse

If you set the Time Lapse setting to its maximum of 10 seconds, you can really have some fun with the Xoom's video capabilities without worrying too much about running out of memory. Approximately 18 seconds of video is taken for every 60 seconds of elapsed time. This means that 10 minutes of real-time action being shot is reduced to about 3 minutes of recorded video.

Using Gallery to View Photos and Video

The Gallery app is where you go to view all the photos and videos that you took with your Xoom.

1. Open the Apps folder and tap the Gallery icon.

2. Videos and photos taken with the Xoom are in the Camera folder.

3. Any images or videos you down-loaded are in the Download folder.

4. Tap the Camera folder to open it.

5. Thumbnails of your photos and videos appear.

6. Videos have the small Play icon in the center.

7. Tap the Slideshow button to watch a slideshow of all photos and the first frame of any videos.

8. Tap the Video/Photo toggle but-ton to choose between displaying videos only, photos only, or both.

9. Tap the Information button and then a video or photo to view detailed information, such as time the file was created, file size, and more.

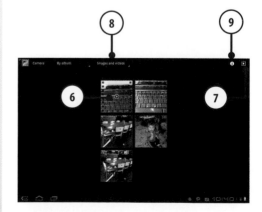

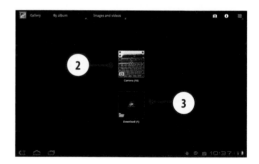

Sharing a Digital Photo or Video via Gmail

You can easily share photos and videos (if they're not too large in size) with email. Within an email, you can always browse the Gallery by electing to add an attachment (see Chapter 5, "Using Email") but there's an easier way to do so while you're actually viewing your photos and videos.

1. Open the Gallery app and select a photo to display.

2. Tap the Share button.

3. Select Gmail (or Email).

4. The Gallery app opens a blank email message.

5. Enter the recipient email address(es).

6. Type the subject of your email.

7. Compose your message.

8. Tap the Send button to send the email.

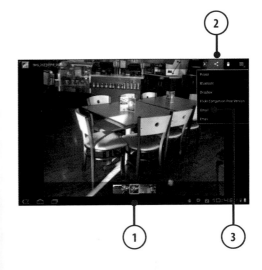

File Size Limits

Gmail users can send and receive messages with attachments of up to 10MB (megabytes) in size, but not all email accounts allow files this large. Some email services limit attachments to 5MB or less. This means that you should send only the shortest of videos as email attachments. At maximum picture size of 5 megapixels, a photo taken with the Xoom's camera produces a 1.2MB file. At this size, it's best to limit emails to no more than one or two photo attachments at a time.

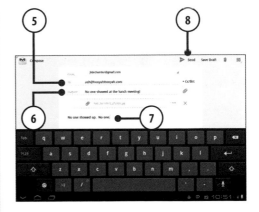

Posting a Digital Photo or Video with Flickr

If you have a Flickr account, it's super simple to upload a digital photo or video to the cloud-based photo-sharing service. (If you don't have a Flickr account, you can get a free account at www.flickr.com.) To post a photo or video on Flickr, follow these steps:

1. Open the Browser app to www.flickr.com.

2. Tap the Sign In button.

3. Log in with a Yahoo! ID, a Facebook, or a Google user account.

4. Tap the Upload Photos & Video button. Be patient; it might take a minute or so for the Flickr loader screen to appear.

5. Tap a Choose File button.

6. Select Gallery.

7. Browse the Camera, Download, or other folders, and tap a photo to choose it. You can select up to six photos or videos, one per Upload button.

Other Options for Flickr

In addition to selecting photos and videos from the Gallery app, you can also select the Camera or Camcorder options; either of these opens the Camera app and enables you to take a photo or shoot a video that you can then upload to Flickr. Photos and videos taken using this method are stored in the Gallery app.

8. Tag your photos or videos with text descriptions, if desired.

9. Tap the Upload button.

10. Your photo and videos are uploaded and available for viewing using the Flickr service.

11. Add more tags for the photos and videos you uploaded.

12. You can change the title of the videos/photos by entering your own text in the Title field for each image.

13. Click the Save button.

Understanding Flickr

By default, Flickr makes your photos and videos available for viewing to the entire world. If you want to make your photos and videos viewable only to certain people—friends and family, for example—you need to spend some time reading over the Help documentation and configuring various security settings. Flickr has many more features available than can be covered here, so I highly encourage you to spend some time exploring on the site.

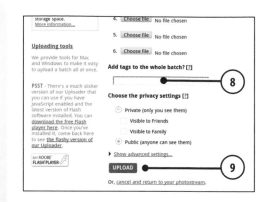

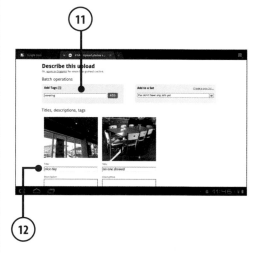

14. Your photos and videos are displayed on your Flickr account screen.

15. Upload more videos and photos, if desired.

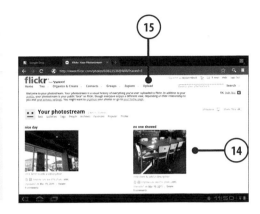

Posting a Digital Video to YouTube

Another great way to share your digital videos is via YouTube, which is the world's largest and most well-known digital video-sharing site. It's free to upload videos, but it requires a user account (you can use your Google account or create one specifically for use with YouTube), so visit www.youtube.com and create an account before uploading any videos.

1. Open a digital video in the Gallery app.

2. Tap anywhere on the screen and tap the Share button.

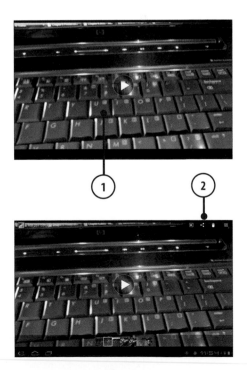

3. Select the YouTube option.

4. Provide a title for the video.

5. Tap the Upload button to begin the upload.

6. An alert informs you when the upload is completed.

7. Open the Browser app to www.youtube.com and log in.

8. Your uploaded video appears and can be played by tapping the icon.

Understanding YouTube

As with Flickr, any videos you upload are, by default, available for viewing by anyone in the world. You can make your videos private, prevent commenting, and much more, but it requires some tweaking of your YouTube account. Consult YouTube's help files for more information on security and how to configure it for your account.

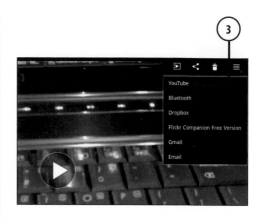

Search the Android Market for the best apps—games, education, business, books, and more.

In this chapter, you learn how to use the Android Market, an online marketplace for downloading free apps. You learn how to purchase fee-based apps and how to uninstall apps and perform updates.

7

The Android Market

Your Xoom comes standard with a dozen or more apps, such as Gallery, Camera, and Email. There are many apps that you'll find yourself using daily and others that you might never use. There might be a task or function that you'd like to perform with your Xoom that the preloaded apps simply do not offer.

Fortunately, the Xoom does not limit you to just those preloaded apps. Thousands of apps are available for the Xoom, some free and some not-so-free, and all you have to do to get them is pay a visit to the Android Market, a "one-stop shop" for Android apps to run on your Xoom.

Exploring the Android Market

Knowing what type of app you want to install is helpful, but not necessary. The Android Market provides categories that can help you narrow your search and just browse what others are finding useful or fun.

1. Tap to open the Apps folder.

2. Tap the Market app to open it.

3. Apps of interest scroll across the top of the screen; tap one to jump to that app's information screen.

4. Tap Featured Tablet Apps to view a list of the Top 48 apps that other Android users find useful, fun, and interesting. (Keep in mind that some apps might appear small in size when opened—this likely means the app was designed for a mobile phone and not the Xoom.)

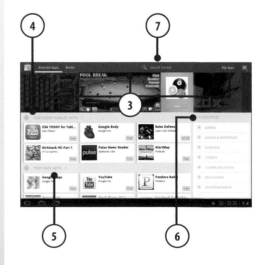

5. Tap Top Free Apps to view the thousands of free apps that are rated highly (more than four stars out of five), or have a high number of downloads (typically in the range of 50,000 or more).

6. Tap a category to view apps of interest. Each category is also broken into sections, such as Featured, Top Free, and Best Selling.

7. Tap the Search Market text field. This is useful if you know the name of an app or a keyword that might be associated with it.

Don't Use Category Names as Keywords

Rather than typing in "racing games" for a keyword search, use the Games category instead. Using a category provides more refined results, whereas using a keyword simply provides you with results that contain either of the two words; you might find business or reference apps that have the word "racing" in their descriptions but are not games.

Examining an App's Information Page

Before you download and install any app to your Xoom, read the app's information page. Reading an app's description can help you determine whether the app meets your needs, inform you about any fees associated with it (there are one-time fees and recurring fees), and provide you with screenshots and customer reviews.

1. From the Android Market, tap an app in either the Featured Tablet Apps category or the Top Free Apps category. (In this example, I tapped on the USA Today for Tablets app.)

2. You can see the price of an app (or if it's free).

3. You can find the version number and app size.

4. You can read a description of the app.

5. Tap the More button to read additional description content.

6. Scroll down the page to view more information.

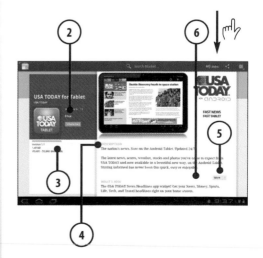

7. Read the What's New section to see what has been changed or fixed since the last version of the app was released.

8. View screenshots. Swipe your finger left or right to view additional screenshots that might be off the screen.

9. Read reviews from other customers and see reviewers' ratings (out of five stars).

10. You might need to scroll down the page to view additional information.

11. Tap the More button to read more customer reviews.

12. View related apps. These are suggested apps provided by the Android Market based on other customer purchases and reviews.

13. Tap the More button to view additional apps that Android Market recommends.

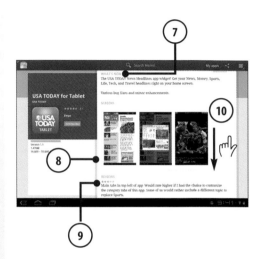

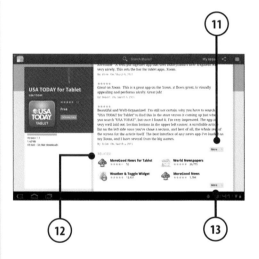

Ratings Can Be Confusing

Because the Android Market averages the star ratings, it can be difficult to determine an app's true value. If there are 20 reviews, 10 one-star and 10 five-star, the average three-star review doesn't really help. This is where reading the customer reviews on the app really makes a difference. Reading a five-star review that says, "Great app," and a one-star review that says, "Here are ten things that aren't working in this app," really helps you make a decision on whether it's worth it to download the app.

Downloading a Free App

If you find an app that you like and it's free, you can immediately download it to your Xoom and begin using it.

1. From the app's information page, tap the Download button.

2. For both free and fee-based apps, you see a pop-up window letting you know what services the app requires to work.

Read the Service Requirements Carefully

Some apps only require an Internet connection (called Network Communication) and memory storage space. Other apps require things such as your GPS location, your Contacts database, and more. Always ask yourself, "Why does this game require access to my contacts or need to know where I am right now?" Sometimes the answer is that the company is collecting email addresses and wants to know your location for marketing purposes. It can bundle this information and sell it to marketers. But this isn't always the case—some apps (such as GPS-related apps) simply need access to your location to function properly. It can be a bit difficult to determine the reasons an app needs access to certain information, but in general you need to be more suspicious with the free apps than with with fee-based apps. Ultimately, it's your call whether to accept the requirements or not.

3. Tap the OK button to proceed with the download, or tap Cancel to opt out of the download.

4. If you click OK, you see a message indicating that the installation has started.

5. After the installation is complete, click the Open button to open the app and use it.

6. Tap the Manage button.

7. Place a checkmark in the check-box if you want to allow an app to perform automatic updates (optional). (See the "Automatic Updating" note for details on why you might not want certain apps to automatically update.)

8. Tap the Open button to open the app and use it.

9. Tap the Uninstall button to remove the app from your Xoom.

Uninstall Doesn't Mean You Must Repurchase

If you choose to uninstall an app that you've purchased, the record of that purchase transaction is saved by Google. This means should you ever want to reinstall that app, you won't have to buy it again. There is one exception: Should you purchase an app, install it, and then request a refund (within the 15-minute time limit), you have to buy the app again if you want to reinstall.

Automatic Updating

Allowing an app to automatically download and install updates sounds like a nice feature, but be careful. By enabling this feature, you are basically allowing the web developer to make changes to the app, including giving it access to information, such as contacts and GPS location, without informing you. Your Xoom automatically notifies you when an app has an update, and updating manually is such an easy thing to do (I show you how to do it shortly) that I recommend against the automatic update feature.

It's Not All Good

FREE DOESN'T ALWAYS MEAN FREE

Just because an app doesn't cost anything to download, it doesn't mean that the app is truly free to use. Many apps (especially games) can be downloaded for free, but then have either a recurring monthly cost associated with them or offer what are called *in-app purchases* and *unlocks*. Examples of monthly costs include digital magazine subscriptions (where the app is simply a container to hold issues) or subscriptions to play games such as MMOGs (Massive Multiplayer Online Games), where hundreds or thousands of players are online and playing with or against you. Examples of in-app purchases and unlocks include special weapons in games that only those who pay have access to (and typically give that player an advantage) and features that are visible to the user, but are disabled until a fee is paid to unlock that ability. Read an app's information page carefully to determine whether there are any actual fees required to use a "free" app.

Downloading a Fee-Based App

Not all apps are free—some have a one-time cost and others have recurring fees. But if you find an app that you really like and must own, buying it is super simple.

1. On the app's information page, tap the Buy button, which automatically launches the Google Checkout screen (it's the official method for purchasing apps from the Android Market).

2. On the Google Checkout screen, provide all the requested information.

3. Place a checkmark in the check-box to acknowledge that you have read and understand Google's Terms & Conditions.

4. Scroll to the bottom of the page.

5. Tap the Save and Continue button to make your purchase, or click the Cancel button to stop the purchase.

6. Click the OK button to accept the service requirements for the app.

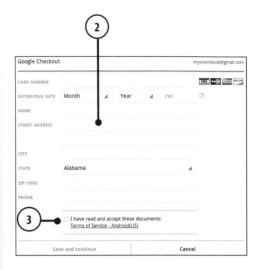

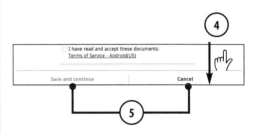

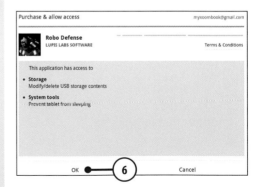

7. The app installs as Google Checkout completes the transaction.

8. Click the Open button to open the app.

9. Click the Manage button to uninstall or configure automatic updates.

The 15-Minute Refund

After you make an app purchase with Google Checkout, you have a 15-minute window of opportunity to open the app, try it out, and decide if you want to keep it. Before those 15 minutes expire, if you decide you don't like the app, you can get a refund by visiting the app's information page (open Android Market and search for the app name) and tapping the Manage button. If time hasn't expired, tap the Uninstall & Refund button to get your money back.

Updating an App

Many app developers are constantly working to improve their apps by fixing bugs and adding new features. When an app developer releases an update to an app you have, an alert notification appears onscreen (unless you configure your apps to automatically update). You can click the alert to immediately begin the update, but if you don't have time, there's another method for updating at your convenience.

1. While in the Android Market, search for the name of the app you want to update.

2. Open the app's information page.

3. Tap the Update button.

Some Updates Are for Paid Versions Only

Many apps are available as a free, try-it-before-you-buy-it version. Although the free versions can be a great way to try out an app, many app developers only release updates for the fee-based versions.

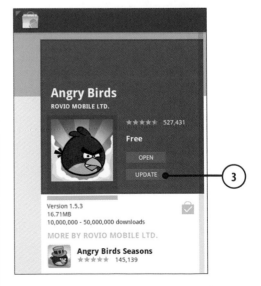

4. Tap the OK button if you agree to the services required by the app, or tap Cancel to stop the update.

5. The update is installed.

6. Tap the Open button to run the updated app.

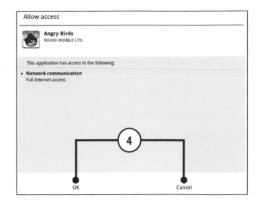

Uninstalling an App

There are two methods for uninstalling an app. You saw that the first way to uninstall an app is to tap the Manage button on an installed app's information page and select Uninstall. The second method is done using the Settings screen.

1. Open the Apps folder.

2. Tap Settings.

3. Select Applications.

4. Tap Manage Applications.

5. Tap the Downloaded option to view apps that did not come pre-installed on your Xoom.

6. Scroll down the list and tap on an app to uninstall it.

7. Tap the Uninstall button.

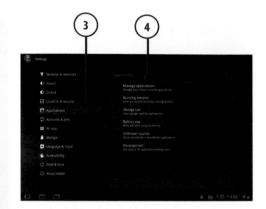

8. Tap the OK button to confirm the uninstall operation, or tap the Cancel button to stop the uninstall of the app.

9. Tap the OK button to close the notification window.

10. The app is uninstalled and removed from the Apps folder. Any data associated with an uninstalled app (such as a game file that stores high scores) is also deleted from the Xoom.

Checking App Storage Use

Your Xoom comes with a lot of memory (32GB), and an SD card enables you to add even more memory. But over time, as you install apps, movies, books, and music, you're going to want to keep an eye on your available storage. Apps are not typically large in size, but there's an easy way to look at all of your apps' storage requirements and see how much memory is left. If you find memory getting tight, consider uninstalling some of the larger apps that you don't use very often.

1. Open the Apps folder and tap Settings.

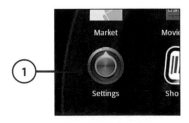

2. Tap Applications.

3. Select the Storage Use option.

4. Tap the Downloaded category to view all apps not preinstalled on your Xoom.

5. Scroll down the list.

6. Each app's size (in megabytes) is displayed below the app's name.

7. Total storage space is displayed.

8. Storage space used is displayed.

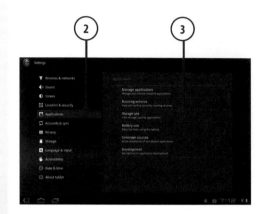

Be Careful When Uninstalling Apps

You can always uninstall apps that you downloaded and installed, but you can also uninstall many of the preloaded apps that came with your Xoom. But, be careful—by selecting the All category while viewing the list of app sizes, you'll see a lot of apps with names that might not be familiar to you. Many of these apps are system apps required by the Android operating system, and uninstalling them might cause your Xoom to stop working properly. When in doubt, remember that if the app can be found in the Android Market, it can most likely be safely removed.

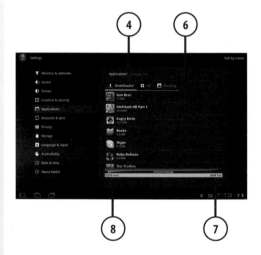

Resetting an App

Many apps save user data over time. The most obvious example is a game where high scores or the current level you are playing is saved until you play the game again. Other apps can save data, such as credit card info, addresses, and phone numbers. You can easily reset an app, making it "forget" whatever configuration and data are saved.

1. Open the Apps folder and tap Settings.

2. Tap Applications.

3. Select the Manage Applications option.

4. Select the Downloaded category.

5. Tap an app. (In this example, I select Angry Birds.)

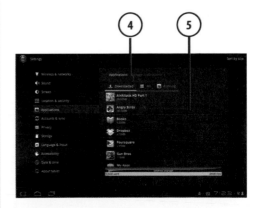

6. See how much data the app is storing.

7. Tap the Clear Data button. (If the button is grayed out, there is no data to delete or the app does not allow it.)

8. Click the OK button to confirm the data deletion, or click the Cancel button to cancel the data deletion.

9. The amount of data stored is cleared.

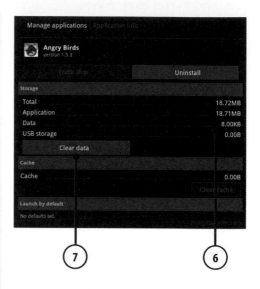

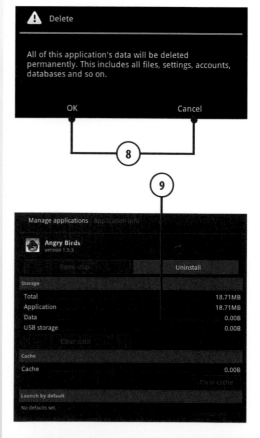

Downloading Non-Android Market Apps

Apps are appearing everywhere, not just in the Android Market. Although the Android Market is considered the official place for obtaining apps for your Xoom, it's not the only place. App developers do not have to make their apps available for download via the Android Market, so if you ever find a site that offers Android apps (such as Amazon.com), you need to configure your Xoom to allow it to download apps from these third-party app providers.

1. Open the Apps folder and click Settings.

2. Tap Applications.

3. Select the Unknown Sources option.

4. Tap OK to acknowledge that you understand the risks to your Xoom from third-party apps, or tap Cancel to prevent your Xoom from downloading apps from sources outside of the Android Market.

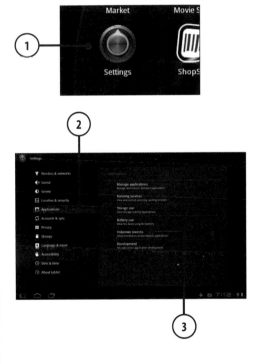

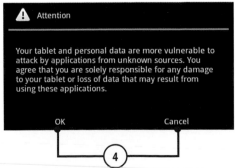

5. A checkmark is placed in the
    checkbox to remind you that
    third-party non-Android Market
    apps can be installed.

Android Market App Testing

Supposedly, all apps that are
made available for download via
the Android Market have been
tested and evaluated to help
identify any apps that could damage (intentionally or not) your
Xoom. This damage could come
from simply poor development
standards, or it could be inten-
tional from a developer who
doesn't have your Xoom's best
interest in mind. As more Android
app markets become available,
you'll have to do your research
and determine the risks; sites such
as Amazon.com, for example, are
likely to have their own form of
testing and evaluation and can
probably be considered safe. Do
your homework and download all
apps with caution.

Use the built-in GPS to get directions to gas, ATMs, restaurants, and other desired destinations.

In this chapter, you learn how to use the Xoom's GPS feature with the Navigation app, including getting directions via the Speak Destination and Type Destination tools. You also learn about Places and how easy it is to use to find specific services, such as gas, ATMs, and more.

8

→ Using Navigation

→ Seeing Where You Are

→ Speaking Your Destination

→ Typing Your Destination

→ Checking Traffic Conditions

→ Finding Food, Gas, and an ATM

→ Avoiding Tollbooths and Highways

→ Taking a Stroll Instead

GPS and Navigation

With Xoom's GPS capabilities, you never have to worry about getting lost between current location A and destination B. Using the built-in Navigation app that's built on Google Maps, you can get driving and walking directions, view up-to-the-minute traffic conditions, and find gas stations, stores, restaurants, ATMs, and more.

Using Navigation

The Navigation app is the perfect tool for getting directions, finding amenities, and seeing what kinds of traffic conditions lay ahead. It doesn't overload
you with features, either. With the Xoom's big screen, you'll find using the
Navigation app an enjoyable experience compared to the squinting required
to read street names on standard GPS devices.

1. Open the Apps folder.

2. Tap the Navigation app to open it.

3. The Navigation user interface
   screen opens.

4. Tap to switch between driving
   and walking directions.

5. Tap to speak your destination. You
   can say a street address, for example, or a city and state name.

6. Tap to type your destination. Use
   the onscreen keyboard to provide
   details of your destination.

7. Tap to view contacts associated
   with starred locations or other
   addresses you provide.

8. Select the Map option to immediately view your current location.

9. You can tap the Route Options
   button to avoid tollbooths or
   highways.

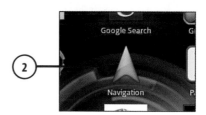

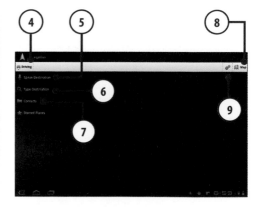

Google Maps

The Xoom comes with the Maps app, which enables you to access Google Maps to search for stores, read reviews, and, of course, get directions (via car, walking, bus, and bicycle). But, Google Maps doesn't provide real-time driving directions using the Navigation's Voice Assistant, which can help you focus on your driving and the road instead of looking at a screen. Google Maps offers a lot more features than Navigation, but it's simply not as good a solution for getting directions from A to B as the Navigation app.

Seeing Where You Are

Before you get driving or walking directions from your current location, it's a good idea to actually see whether the Navigation app is aware of your current location.

1. Open the Navigation app and tap the Map button.

2. After the Navigation app is determines your location, it displays a blue indicator arrow in the center of the screen.

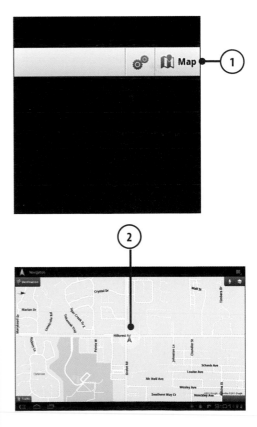

3. Use your thumb and pointer finger to pinch on the screen to zoom out to see a wider area.

4. Use a reverse-pinch (placing your thumb and pointer finger together on the screen and then moving them apart) to zoom in.

5. While tapping and holding on the screen, drag your finger to move the onscreen map.

6. The blue arrow representing your location moves away from the center of the screen and might even disappear if you drag the map too far from your current location.

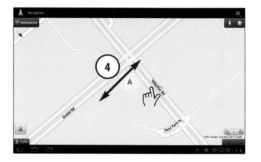

7. Tap the Center Location button to always place your current location back in the center of the screen.

8. You can use the Zoom In and Zoom Out buttons to zoom in and out instead of using pinching and reverse-pinching gestures.

Bird's Eye View

When using the Map feature of Navigation, you are viewing your location from a bird's eye view—directly from above. Street names are displayed if you're not zoomed out too far; otherwise, only highway and interstate numbers are visible.

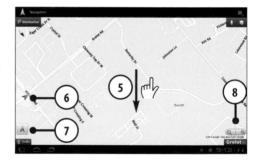

Speaking Your Destination

Now, it's time to get some directions. The easiest way to use Navigation is to simply speak your destination. You must speak clearly; otherwise, Navigation might resolve your destination incorrectly. If that happens, simply try again. (If you find that speaking the destination isn't working, you can always type it in—read more in the next section.)

1. Open the Navigation app and tap the Speak Destination button.

Use the Search-Speak Option

If you're not currently running the Navigation app but want to get directions, you can also tap the Search-Speak button on the home screen. Say "Navigate To" followed by your destination and the Navigation app automatically opens and provides the requested directions.

2. If you are already using the Maps feature of Navigation, tap the small microphone icon button.

3. The Speak Now window appears.

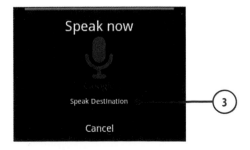

Voice Recognition Isn't Perfect

The voice recognition feature isn't always perfect. It can have difficulty resolving complicated street names and often tries to find the closest match. When speaking address numbers, it's best to speak each number individually— say "five-six-zero-five Main Street" instead of "fifty-six-oh-five Main Street," for example. If Navigation has difficulty, it might pop up a window onscreen with options, asking you to tap the correct selection. If you find using voice navigation frustrating, you're not alone. There are still some bugs to work out, but there's always the option of typing your destination.

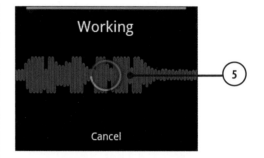

4. Speak your destination.

5. Navigation attempts to resolve your destination.

6. Navigation resolves your destination. Tap Go to start receiving directions to your destination.

7. You hear the Voice Assistant speak your destination and give you the first set of directions ("Drive 100 feet and make a U-turn on to Hillcrest Road", for example.)

8. A blue line indicates the route you should drive.

9. U-turns are indicated.

10. Tap the current street name and the Navigation app centers your current location onscreen.

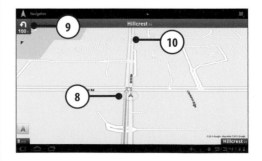

11. You can view the next set of instructions by tapping the Next arrow.

12. Distance to the next turn is provided along with a left or right direction (turning right in two miles, for example).

13. Tap the Previous arrow to return to the previous set of instructions.

14. Tap the Then arrow to view the next set of instructions.

15. Tap the Text Instructions button.

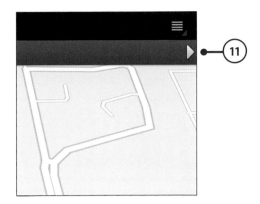

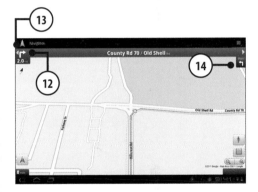

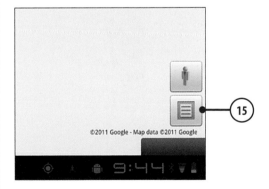

16. A complete set of instructions becomes available.

17. Total distance and estimated time to destination is provided.

18. Tap the Return button to go back to the Map View.

19. Tap the Street View button.

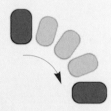

20. The screen rotates to give you a view of your current location as viewed from your vehicle. Street View is useful for finding visual landmarks, such as buildings.

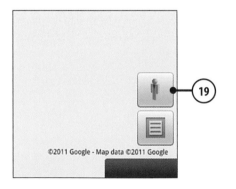

21. Press the Toggle button to return to the Map View.

22. Your destination is represented by this icon.

23. The final destination is displayed along the top of the screen.

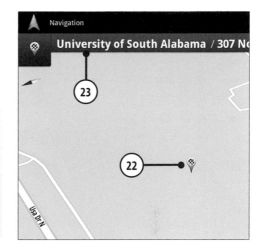

It's Not All Good

STREET VIEW ISN'T PERFECT EITHER

The Street View feature is currently a beta feature offered by Google. *Beta* means it's in testing, and the verdict is still out on whether it will become a permanent feature. The resolution of the images is low quality (currently) and although Street View is helpful for finding landmarks, it's not all that useful when driving. Instead, consider it an option when walking.

Typing Your Destination

Instead of speaking your destination, you can type it using the onscreen keyboard. After typing the destination, the Navigation app works in the same manner as if you'd spoken your destination.

1. Open the Navigation app and tap the Type Destination button.

2. Use the onscreen keyboard to enter the destination.

3. Tap the Return button when done.

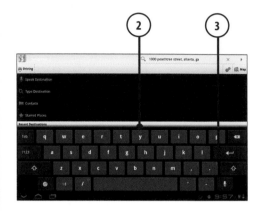

4. If Navigation is unable to resolve the address, it might offer alternatives. Tap the correct address if it is listed or check the address and re-enter it.

5. The address is resolved, and Navigation provides you with the total miles and estimated travel time.

6. Follow the instructions provided by the Voice Assistant or use the text instructions (refer to the previous section).

Roads with Similar Names

Don't make the mistake I did and assume that the Navigation app will select the correct street. In Atlanta, Georgia, there are dozens of streets that start with the word "Peachtree," and the Navigation app seems to always want to default to one particular road. Whenever possible, type the destination instead of using the voice option just to be sure.

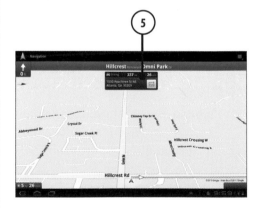

Checking Traffic Conditions

The Navigation app offers you the ability to get a bird's eye view of traffic along your route. This helps you see what's ahead (if you're already in your car and driving), or it alerts you to problems ahead and allows you to find an alternate route.

1. While using the Navigation app, use the pinch gesture to zoom out.

2. Local roads appear white in color.

3. While zoomed out, roads where traffic is moving at posted speeds are shown in green.

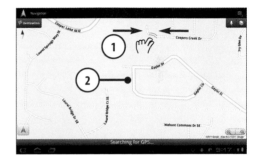

4. Roads where traffic is moving slower than posted speeds are shown in yellow.

5. Roads where traffic is stopped or a serious accident or road work is being performed will typically be shown in red.

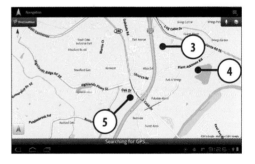

Traffic Information Not Available Everywhere

Although Google does its best to collect traffic data from every location it can, not every city and town makes this information available. The only way to know for sure is to check the Navigation app and see whether traffic speeds show up. If the roads in your current area only show the standard white color with no yellows, greens, or reds, it's likely that Google is unable to obtain traffic data for your current location.

6. If traffic data is not shown on the screen, tap the Layers button.

7. On the Layers screen, tap the Traffic View option.

8. If traffic data is available, it displays as an overlay over the current Map View.

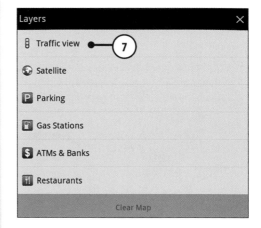

Finding Food, Gas, and an ATM

You can easily configure the Navigation app to show you various amenities in your area and along your route. These include parking facilities, gas stations, ATMs and banks, and restaurants.

1. While the Navigation app is in Map View, tap the Layers button.

2. Tap the Gas Stations option.

3. Small icons appear on the map, indicating where gas can be purchased.

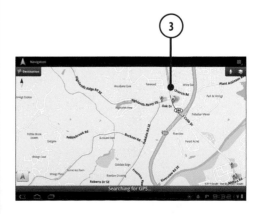

4. Tap the Layers button again.

5. Tap the ATMs & Banks option.

6. Tap the Layers button again. (You need to tap the Layers button for each option you want to select.)

7. Select the Restaurants option.

8. Gas stations are represented by a small gas pump icon.

9. ATMs are visible with small $ signs as icons.

10. Restaurants are indicated by a small fork-and-knife icon.

11. Tap a restaurant icon once to see its name. Tap the restaurant icon a second time.

12. Click to get the restaurant's phone number; this is useful for making reservations.

13. Click the Directions button to get directions to the restaurant from your current location.

14. Tap the More Info option to get reviews, details about the cuisine, and more.

15. Tap the Map button to return to the Map View.

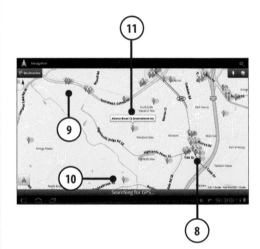

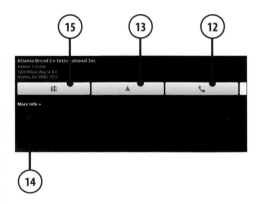

Avoiding Tollbooths and Highways

When driving to a specific location, you might want to avoid tollbooths and/or highways.

1. Open the Navigation app to the Menu screen.

2. Tap the Settings button.

3. Select the Avoid Highways option to disallow highways and interstates from being included in the directions.

4. Tap the Avoid Tolls option to prevent tollbooths from being included in directions.

5. Tap the OK button to apply your selection(s).

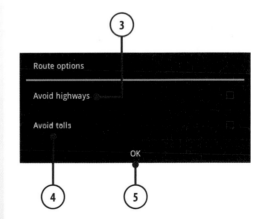

Finding a Way Around Stopped Traffic

The Navigation app often includes highways and interstates on a route because they provide a shorter travel time; this can cause problems, however, if a highway or interstate is stopped due to construction or an accident. By disallowing Navigation to use highways, you can obtain an alternate route by exiting the highway and allowing Navigation to find a shortcut to bypass the construction or accident.

Your Xoom becomes a portable library with the best eBook services available as apps.

In this chapter, you learn how to buy, download, and read eBooks on your Xoom. You learn about two apps, Kindle and Google Books, that give you access to more books than you can find in any bricks-and-mortar bookstore.

9

Reading an eBook

Your Xoom provides you with Internet browsing, email, maps and directions, and a digital camera, but there's still much more it can do! Digital books and music are all the rage these days, and your Xoom is fully capable of offering you the ability to read a digital book (eBook) and listen to music. With its large storage capacity, you can literally carry your personal library of books and music wherever you roam.

Installing Kindle

Many eBook readers are available, and one of the most popular is the Kindle app from Amazon.com. When you purchase an eBook from Amazon, it's available on any device you own that can run the Kindle app, including laptops, mobile phones, home computers…and yes, your Xoom. But, before you can read an eBook, you need to download and install the free Kindle app.

1. Open the Apps folder and tap the Market app.

2. Use the search bar and type **Kindle**.

3. Tap the Return key when done.

4. Tap the Kindle app in the search results page.

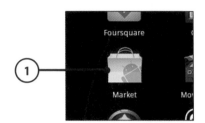

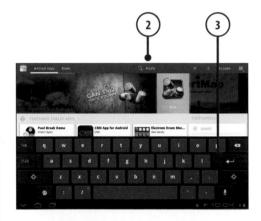

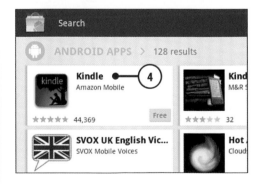

5. Tap the Download button.

6. Tap the OK button. The Kindle app installs; this might take a minute or so.

7. Tap the Open button to open the Kindle app.

The App Is Free

The Kindle app is free…it's the eBooks that typically cost you. Although Amazon.com offers a handful of free eBook downloads (typically classic novels that are available on the Internet elsewhere for free), most of the eBooks on Amazon.com cost you anywhere from $0.99 to $13.99. Think of the Kindle app simply as a folder where you store your Amazon.com eBook purchases.

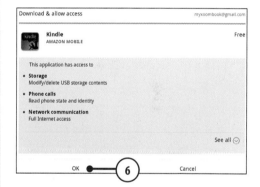

Registering with Amazon.com

The first time you open and use Kindle, you need to register by providing an email address and password. This registration is how Amazon.com tracks your purchases and enables you to view your eBooks on other devices (such as a mobile phone or laptop) without having to repurchase them.

1. Open the Kindle app.

2. Enter your email address and password if you already have an Amazon.com account.

3. Tap the Don't Have an Amazon.com Account button if you need to create an Amazon.com account. (For this section, I'm tapping this button and creating an account.)

4. Enter your name, email address, and a password.

5. Tap the Create Account button.

6. Tap the Remember button if you want the Browser app to remember your login credentials and automatically log you into Amazon.com.

7. Tap the Never button if you want to enter your username and password every time you access Amazon.com.

8. Tap the Not Now button and you are prompted again the next time you access Amazon.com. (I select this option for now.)

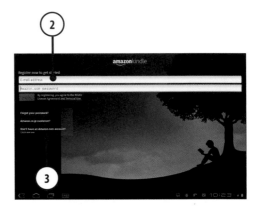

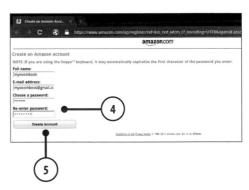

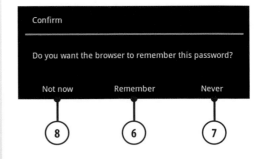

9. Your account is created.

10. Tap the Return to Kindle for Android button.

11. Type your email address and password.

12. Tap the Register button.

13. The Kindle eBook browser screen opens.

14. A few free eBooks are ready for you to open and read.

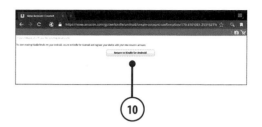

Free eBooks Might Change

From time to time, Amazon changes the free eBooks that are available in the Kindle app. Don't worry—in the next section, I show you how to find all the free eBooks that Kindle makes available, and you can download any of them…or all of them!

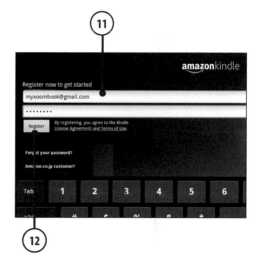

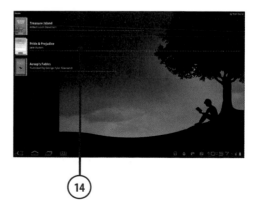

Downloading a Free eBook

With the Kindle app, you can purchase and download many books. But, Amazon.com also offers a nice list of free eBooks. Browse the list, find a book you want to read, and download it at no cost. You've already seen that a few free eBooks are loaded into the Kindle app, but you also need to know where to go to find all the free eBooks that Amazon.com makes available.

1. Open the Kindle app to the eBook browser screen.

2. Tap the Menu button.

3. Tap the Kindle Store button.

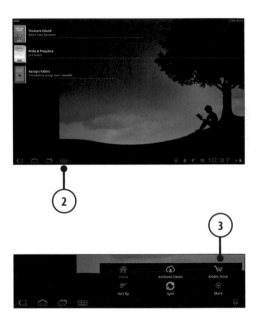

Other Menu Options

Besides accessing the Kindle Store, the Menu button also enables you to sort your eBooks by title, author, and other criteria. The Sync button checks your Amazon.com account to see whether you have made any eBook purchases from another device (such as a mobile phone) and automatically downloads new eBooks to the Xoom if any are found.

4. The Kindle Store search tool opens.

5. Tap the Free Popular Classics button.

6. Browse the list of free eBooks; ten titles per page are displayed.

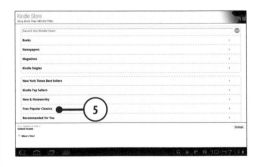

7. Tap a book to open its information page.

8. Tap the Show More Results to view the next ten titles.

9. The free eBook's information page opens.

10. Read reviews from other readers.

11. Verify the price; this eBook is free with a Kindle price of $0.00.

12. Tap the Buy Now with 1-Click button.

13. Enter your email address and password. (This might not appear if you chose to have the Browser app remember your Amazon.com password.)

14. Tap the Sign In button; if you are asked if you want to have your password saved, make a selection.

15. Your purchase is complete. (No charge to your credit card is made for the free classic eBooks.)

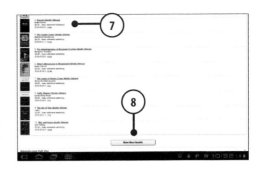

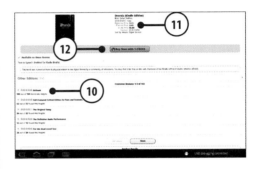

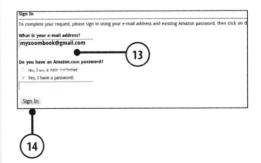

It's Not All Good

AMAZON.COM REQUIRES A CREDIT CARD

For future eBook purchases, you are required to provide a credit card number. The reason for this is that all Kindle app purchases use the Amazon.com feature called 1-Click. 1-Click is just what it sounds like—a single tap on the Buy Now with 1-Click button charges your credit card and immediately downloads your purchase. You don't have to provide standard online purchasing information, such as your address and other details. It's a nice feature, but if you're not comfortable allowing Amazon.com to store your credit card info, the Kindle app is only useful for downloading free eBooks. To provide the credit card info, visit Amazon.com and click the Manage Your Kindle option; there is a link to provide 1-Click credit card information.

16. Tap the Read It Now button to open the eBook.

17. Your new eBook opens, and you can read it in widescreen view.

18. Skip ahead to the section, "Reading an eBook," for instructions on using the eBook reader if you want to start reading right away.

19. Rotate your Xoom to portrait (or vertical) mode to read the eBook with page formatting that matches a traditional book.

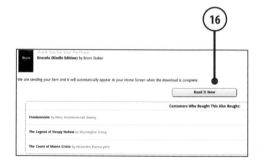

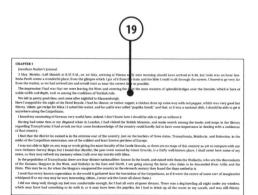

Purchasing an eBook

Free eBooks are great, but eventually, you'll want to download a book that isn't free. Fortunately, with Amazon.com's free 1-Click feature, you can find a book, buy it, download it, and start reading in less than a minute.

1. In the Kindle eBook browser screen, tap the Menu button and select the Kindle Store option.

2. Notice the free eBook downloaded in the previous section now appears on the eBook browser screen.

3. Enter the name of a book you want to learn about and possibly purchase. (In this example, I want to view all the eBooks available in the *Teach Yourself in 10 Minutes* series.)

4. Tap the Go button to begin your search.

5. Books that match your search appear in a list.

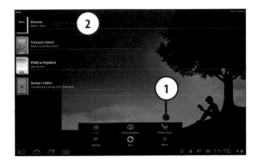

6. Tap a title to view that eBook's information screen.

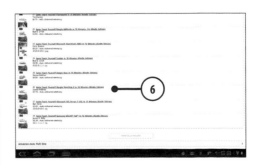

7. Read information about the book (release date, sales ranks, and so on).

8. Tap the Try a Sample button to download a sample chapter or specific number of pages (set by the publisher); this is useful if you want to try it before you buy it.

9. Tap the Buy Now with 1-Click button to purchase the eBook.

10. Your purchase is confirmed.

11. Tap the Read It Now button to open the eBook.

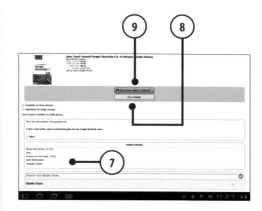

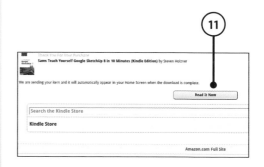

Receipts for Your Purchases

When you make a purchase from Amazon.com, you are sent an email that contains a receipt. This can be useful for books purchased for work (tax write-offs), but it also can alert you if someone is purchasing items from Amazon.com with your user account.

Reading an eBook

Reading an eBook is similar to reading a printed book, but there are no paper pages to turn. After you open an eBook with the Kindle app, you can see that you have more options than simply reading the book. Many special features can make using an eBook reader more enjoyable. For the remainder of this chapter, I use Xoom in vertical mode so that the eBook pages are formatted like a traditional printed book.

1. To turn a page, use a swipe gesture on the screen. Swipe right to left to turn to the next page in an eBook. Swipe left to right to turn to the previous page in an eBook.

Pick Up Where You Left Off

When you tap the Home button on your Xoom, the Kindle app automatically saves the page you are currently reading. The next time you open that eBook, the Kindle app returns you to that page—automatic bookmark!

2. Jump to the Table of Contents by tapping the Menu button.

3. Tap the Go To option.

4. Tap the Table of Contents option. (Select the Cover option to view the eBook's cover, and select the Location option to enter a page location.)

Page Location Is Not the Same as Page Number

If you compare a page from a printed book to that same book viewed on your Xoom, you find that they don't exactly match up. Because of how the Kindle app reformats an eBook's page to fit a screen, page numbers aren't useful because they won't match the page numbers in a printed copy. For this reason, the Kindle app uses a Page Location number. In all honesty, it's not that useful of a feature because the page location numbers tend to run into the thousands, even for a printed book of fewer than 300 pages. Rather than use Page Location to find a specific spot in an eBook, I recommend jumping to the Table of Contents and using its hyperlink feature to jump to a desired location in the eBook.

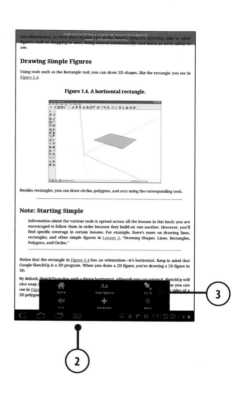

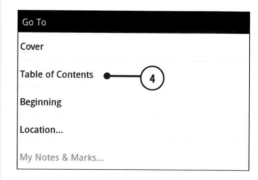

6. The eBook's table of contents appears. Chapters are hyperlinks (as are any book headers or sections), and a single tap on a hyperlink takes you to that spot.

7. Tap a chapter title to jump to the opening page of that chapter.

8. Tap a chapter heading to jump to that particular spot in the eBook. (In this example, I tap the "Painting" section.)

9. The selected location appears on the screen.

10. Tap a blue hyperlinked figure number.

11. The page formatting adjusts so that the selected figure appears at the top of the screen.

View Options Are Universal

When you change the font size, page background color, or the brightness, these settings are saved and applied to your other eBooks stored in the Kindle app. It's worth the effort to spend a few minutes experimenting with these settings and finding what works best for you. You don't have to save the adjustments you make; simply tap anywhere on the eBook's text to close the View Options feature, and the current settings are applied.

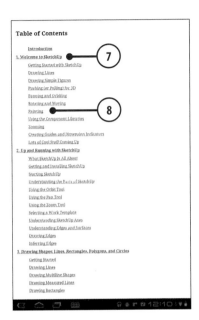

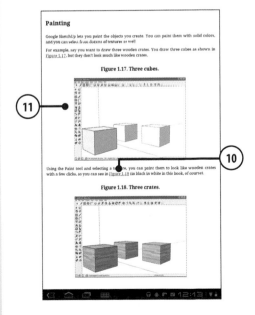

12. Tap the Menu button again.

13. Tap the View Options button.

14. Tap a font size to adjust the size of the onscreen text.

15. Tap a color for the page; white is the default, but sepia is easier on the eyes.

16. Adjust the brightness of the screen by dragging the bar left or right.

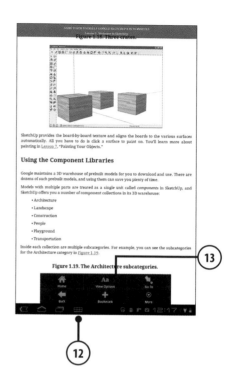

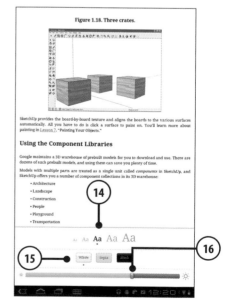

Adding Bookmarks and Notes

When reading an eBook, sometimes you might want to mark a page or passage so you can easily find it later. Although you can't write in the margins of a digital book, you can easily type in notes that are saved when you close an eBook.

1. Open an eBook with the Kindle app.

2. Find a page that you want to bookmark for later reference.

3. Tap the Menu button.

4. Tap the Bookmark button, and the page is bookmarked.

5. Tap and hold your finger on text or a figure on a page until a small toolbar appears.

6. Tap the Note button.

7. Type your note using the onscreen keyboard.

8. Tap the Save button to save your note.

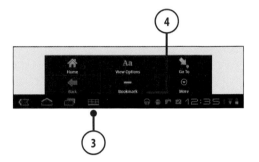

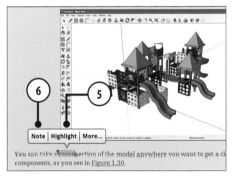

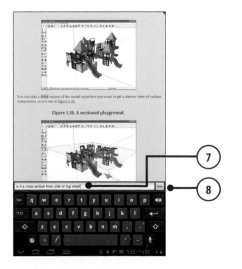

After bookmarks and notes are added, you can easily view them for the current eBook you are reading. To do so, follow these steps:

9. Tap the Menu button.

10. Tap the Go To button.

11. Tap the My Notes & Marks option.

12. Tap a bookmark to jump to that page location.

13. Tap a note to jump to the page where that note was applied.

Bookmarks and Notes Are Universal, Too

If you save a bookmark or note in an eBook stored in the Kindle app, you are also able to access those items while viewing the same eBook on any other device on which you have installed the Kindle app. This means that a note you enter while reading an eBook on your Xoom is accessible when reading the same eBook later on your laptop.

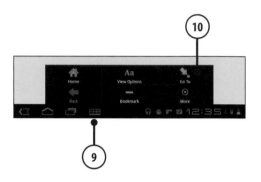

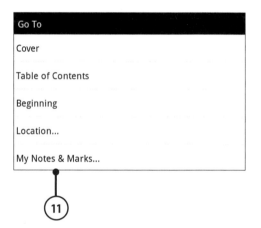

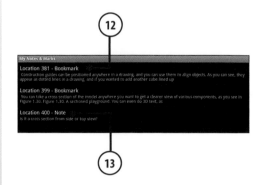

Google Books

Google has an outstanding free eBook reader app. Open the Browser app and point it to books.google.com. Tap the Get the Android App and follow the instructions to download and install it. After the Google Books app is installed, take it for a spin. Google offers books for purchase and more free eBooks than you'll ever have time to read.

1. Open the Google Books app.

2. As with the Kindle app, Google Books offers a few preloaded free eBooks for you to read. Tap a title to open it.

3. Tap the Get eBooks button to open the Google Book Store.

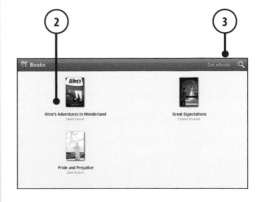

4. When the Google eBooks store opens, you can use the search box to search for author or title or other keywords.

5. Tap a title to view its information page.

6. On a book's information page, tap the price button to purchase (using Google Checkout).

7. Tap the Get Sample button to download a sample chapter or specific number of pages (set by the publisher).

8. Read reviews from other readers.

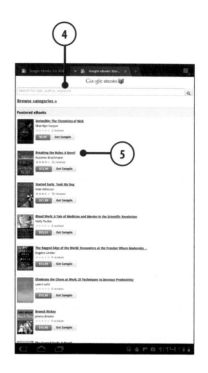

Listen to your favorite artists on the Xoom with the built-in Music app—
browse selections by album, song title, or artist name.

In this chapter, you learn all about using your Xoom to listen to music and news radio. You see how to import and listen to your own music (MP3 files) as well as get an introduction to a free online music service, Pandora.

10

→ Importing Your Music

→ Purchasing Music

→ Listening to Your Music

→ Installing Pandora

→ Using Pandora

Music, Music, Music

The Xoom is an outstanding multimedia device. You've seen how it can be used to read eBooks, and now you discover how the Xoom handles music.

With Music, you can listen to your own music collection that you put together or you can access online music services that stream your favorite styles of music over the Internet and to your Xoom.

Importing Your Music

If you have a nice collection of MP3 files stored on a home computer or laptop, why not copy it over to your Xoom? With your own music files stored on the Xoom, you can listen to your music anytime, anywhere. You can use the built-in speakers (on the back of the Xoom) or plug in your headphones.

1. Plug in your Xoom to the laptop or computer using the USB cable.

2. Click Start.

3. Select Computer (or My Computer).

4. Double-click the Xoom icon.

5. Double-click the Device Storage icon.

6. Notice the approximate storage capacity on the Xoom (30, 182, 852KB, or 30GB).

Works for Both Windows and Mac

The steps in this section are for a Windows Vista laptop, but the steps are almost identical for all other operating systems, including the Mac. When you plug in your Xoom, it's basically visible to your computer as another hard drive, complete with its own folder structure. You can copy files back and forth, but be careful; don't delete or remove any files that you're not familiar with—a safe bet is to only delete files from the Xoom that you actually put there.

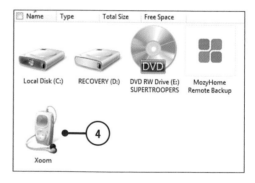

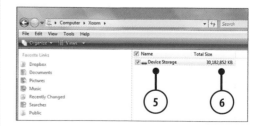

7. The Xoom's file structure is listed.

8. Double-click the Music folder.

9. The Xoom comes preloaded with sample songs.

10. Drag and drop one or more music files into the Music folder. (You can also select multiple MP3 files, right-click and select Copy, and then right-click in the Music folder and select Paste.)

11. The copied song now appears in the Music folder.

12. Open the Apps folder and tap the Music app.

Deleting Music

The easiest method to delete a song is to open the Xoom's File Manager app and delete the song from the Music folder. But if your Xoom is still connected to your computer, just browse to the Xoom's Music folder, and delete the song from there. You can click once on the file and press the Delete key or right-click the file and choose Delete.

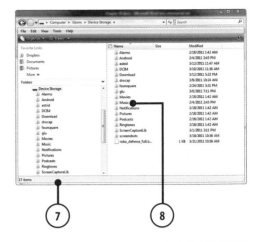

13. Tap the Sort button. (In this example, the New and Recent option is the current selection.)

14. Select the Songs option.

15. Scroll through the complete list of songs stored on the Xoom.

16. The copied MP3 file appears in the list.

Purchasing Music

There are hundreds of websites where you can legally purchase music. Each website probably has a slightly different method for buying and downloading the music, but the idea is the same: Use the Browser app to visit a website where you can buy music and, after locating a song and providing credit card info, allow the Xoom to download the music file and place it automatically in the Music folder. The song is then available using the Music app. For this section, I'm purchasing and downloading a song from Amazon.com.

1. Open the Browser app to www.amazon.com.

2. Select the Search drop-down menu by tapping the small triangle.

3. Scroll down the list of categories.

4. Select the MP3 Downloads option.

5. Enter a song, album, or artist name in the search box.

6. Tap the Go button.

Amazon.com Login Required

If you haven't set the Browser app to remember your email address and password, you might be asked to provide it after tapping the Buy MP3 button.

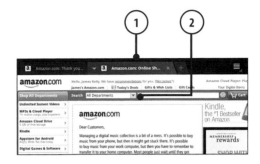

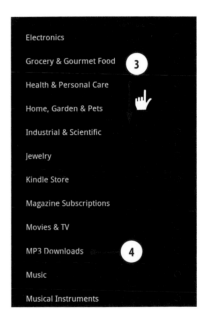

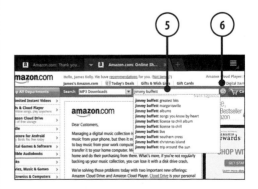

7. Tap an album cover to view the list of songs on that album.

8. Scroll down the list of all music to find a song.

9. Tap the Buy MP3 button to purchase a song.

10. Your selected song is displayed, along with the price.

11. Tap the Continue button.

12. Tap the Save to This Computer button.

13. Don't place a checkmark in the Always Do This checkbox. You might want to purchase music from Amazon.com in the future and use a different storage location or method.

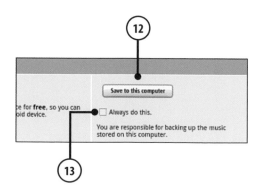

14. Because the Xoom is running the Android operating system, you don't want to install an MP3 downloader. Instead, tap the Skip Installation and Continue link.

15. Tap the Download Song button.

16. Tap the Download Alert icon.

17. A progress bar lets you know how far along the download has progressed. When the download is completed, the song is available to play with the Music app (covered in the next section).

No Download Monitoring

Currently there does not appear to be any kind of download monitoring going on with Android 3.0 (Honeycomb). This is why it's so easy to move, copy, and download files to the Xoom's subfolders. This might change with future updates, but for now just be careful where you download music (and apps in general) to avoid any problems with buggy software or even malicious apps that might seek to damage your Xoom.

Listening to Your Music

Now that you copied some of your music over to the Xoom or purchased a song or two, it's time to listen to some tunes. The Xoom comes with the Music app, which has some nice features that help you organize and play the songs you want to hear.

1. Open the Apps folder and tap on the Music app.

2. Tap the Sort option menu.

3. Select New and Recent to view recently played or downloaded songs.

4. Select the Albums option to sort your music by album name. (For this example, I select this option, which makes all the songs on Xoom sort by their respective albums.)

5. Select the Artists option to sort your music by artist name.

6. Tap the Songs option to list all songs alphabetically.

7. Select the Playlists option to sort music using playlists you defined.

8. Tap the Genres option to organize your music by genre/style.

9. Album covers include title and artist/band name and number of songs in that album that are stored on the Xoom.

10. Tap an Album to open and view its associated songs.

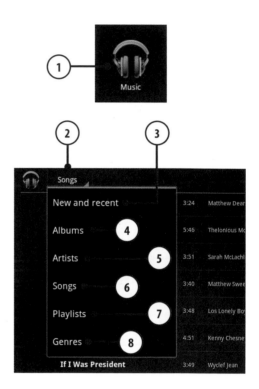

Playlists Defined

The Music app enables you to organize your music using playlists, which you can think of as folders that hold your music that you create and name. The advantage to using playlists is that you can create as many as you like and associate a single song with multiple playlists. For example, you might place a Beatles song into a playlist called "60s Music" as well as "British Faves." Later, if you choose to listen to the 60s Music playlist, you definitely hear that Beatles tune but not, for example, any of John Lennon's 1970s releases that you associated with British Faves.

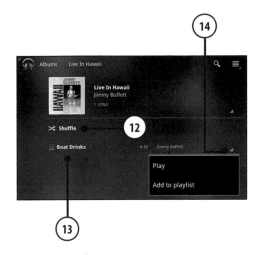

11. The album's songs are listed.

12. If multiple songs are listed, click the Shuffle button to play all the songs in random order.

13. Tap the name of a song to immediately play it.

14. Tap the Options button for a song to either play it or add it to a playlist. (I choose to add the song to a playlist.)

15. Enter a name for a new playlist.

16. Tap the OK button to associate the song with that playlist.

17. Tap the Options button again and select the Add to Playlist option.

18. Tap New Playlist to create a new playlist.

19. Tap an existing playlist to assign to the song.

20. While playing a song, you can tap the Pause button to pause the music. If you tap the Home button and leave the Music app, any music playing continues to play, so tap the Pause button if you don't want background music playing while you access other apps on your Xoom.

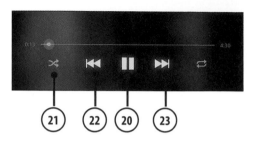

21. Tap the Shuffle button to toggle the shuffle off and on for any remaining songs to be played.

22. Tap the Back button to start the song from the beginning.

23. Tap the Next button to jump to the next song to be played.

24. Tap the Repeat button once to replay all songs currently selected (for example, if you chose a playlist or album).

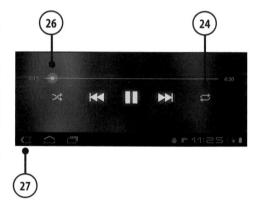

25. Tap the Repeat button a second time to loop the current song and have it play again. (Tap it a third time to turn off the Repeat option.)

26. The song's progress is displayed. You can drag the dot left or right to start playing the song at a desired location.

27. Tap the Return button to return to the selected viewing screen (albums, playlists, or genre, for example).

Other Music Players

Many music players are available from the Android Market. Many are free and some are not. The Music app is a simple music player, but if you're looking for more advanced features and controls, you likely need to find a different app. Use the Music & Audio category to view the most popular and best-selling music-related apps. Winamp is one free, popular choice, and PlayerPro (currently U.S. $4.92) is one of the best-selling players.

Installing Pandora

You can load up your Xoom with your MP3 music files, but another option is to simply play music using your Internet connection. Known as music streaming, you simply use an app to connect to a music service that enables you to search and select music that interests you and then play it through the Xoom. One of the most popular and fun to use is Pandora—and it's 100% free.

1. Open the Android Market and search for Pandora.

2. Select the Pandora Radio app.

3. Tap the Download button to install it. (Review Chapter 7, "The Android Market," for instructions downloading and installing apps from the Android Market.)

4. After installing the Pandora app, click the Open button on the app's information screen or open the Apps folder and tap the Pandora app icon.

5. A warning alerts you to the fact that Pandora can have a major effect on your data charges from your carrier.

6. Tap the Continue button.

7. Create a Pandora user account by tapping the I Am New to Pandora button.

It's Not All Good

STREAMING MUSIC AND SHOCKING BILLS

Pandora is best used if you have an unlimited data plan with your carrier or if your Xoom is currently joined to a Wi-Fi network. If you do not have an unlimited data plan, you could be in for a serious shock when your next bill arrives. Because Pandora is continually downloading data as it plays music, you can easily go over your maximum data allotment in a short time. Rest assured that most data providers are more than happy to charge you for every megabyte of music that you listen to without any warning that you exceeded your limit.

8. Provide the requested information, including email address, password, birth year, and more.

9. Tap the Sign Up button when done.

10. By default, Pandora makes your music selections and searches public. The idea Is that others may discover bands that you're aware of, but they are not. Place a checkmark in the Make My Profile Private checkbox if you do not want your searches and music selections public.

11. Tap the Continue button.

12. Now you're given the opportunity to do your first music request. You can enter the name of an artist, a genre (such as Reggae or Polka), and even a specific song's name. As you type in words, Pandora makes suggestions below the search bar.

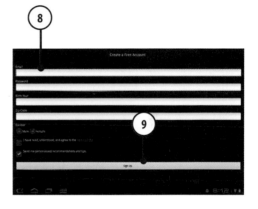

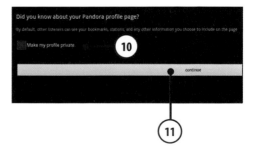

13. Tap a suggestion if you want or leave your search text as it is.

14. Tap the Search button when done.

15. Pandora creates "radio stations" that play the music you search for and music that is similar in sound and style. Your first radio station opens and a song begins to play.

16. Tap the Station button.

17. Your new radio station is listed along with any other radio stations you created.

18. When you have multiple radio stations, tapping one opens and plays it.

19. Tap the Menu button.

20. Tap the Create Station button to add a new station.

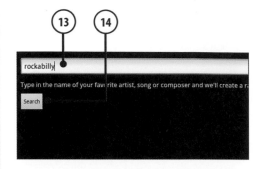

Removing a Radio Station

Sometimes, you grow tired of a specific station and, other times, you find that it's not picking the best matches for the music you really want to listen to; whatever the reason, when you want to remove a station, simply tap and hold on the name of the station until the Delete Station pop-up window appears. Tap Delete Station, and it's gone.

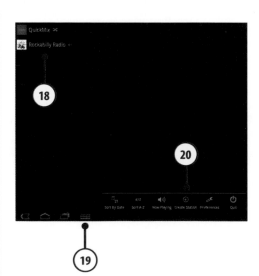

Using Pandora

Pandora's user interface is fairly simple, and it offers you the opportunity to rate songs you hear; it uses your ratings to help refine your station and find the exact type of music you want to hear. Other features include the ability to read information about a favorite artist or album and bookmark a song or artist that you may want to hear more later.

1. While listening to a song, tap the Thumbs Up or Thumbs Down buttons to rate a song.

2. Tap the Next button to end the current song and jump to the next.

3. Tap the Pause button to pause a song.

4. Tap the Information button, which causes details about the artist or band to display.

5. Tap the Song button to read more information about why this song is included with the radio station you selected.

6. Tap the artist/song icon to close the Information screen and return to the song controls.

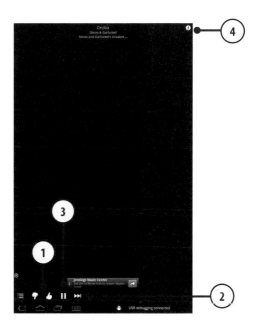

Using a Song's Information to Determine Relevance

Pandora sometimes mixes music styles. Check the information page, and you might find that the lead guitarist of the country band was a member of an 80s rock band. Pandora makes some strange associations, so help Pandora learn about your tastes and what you prefer to hear when you select a radio station by using Thumbs Up and Thumbs Down.

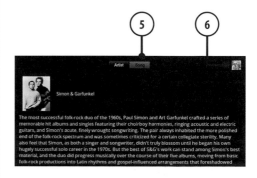

Chat with contacts using Instant Messaging or use the Xoom's built-in webcam for real-time video chats.

In this chapter, you learn how to use your Xoom to have a webcam chat with another Google user using the Talk app. You also learn how to use your Xoom to participate in Instant Messaging sessions with Talk. Finally, you see how to make phone calls using the Skype app.

11

Webcam, Text, and Phone Chats

Your Xoom has a built-in webcam and microphone that makes it a perfect tool for chatting with friends and family over the Internet. You can choose between text-based chats, webcam chats (video and voice), and even phone calls.

Using Google Talk

If Google Talk isn't already installed on your Xoom (it should be), you can find and download it free from the Android Market. After you install the app, all you need to do is log in with your Google user account and password; the app is easy to navigate and all you need to do is configure a few settings before making a webcam call or opening an Instant Messaging session.

1. Open the Apps folder.

2. Tap the Talk app.

3. Talk automatically detects any Google accounts stored on the Xoom.

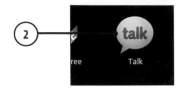

4. Tap the Sign In button. (If you have only one Google user account stored on the Xoom, Talk might automatically log you in.)

5. Your contacts appear in a list.

6. A green icon indicates that person is Available.

7. An orange icon indicates that person is Away.

8. A red icon indicates the user is busy.

9. A gray icon with an X indicates a user is signed out.

10. For each color, there is also an icon shape; a video camera indicates the user has webcam capability, a microphone indicates voice chat, and a solid dot indicates text chat (also called Instant Messaging).

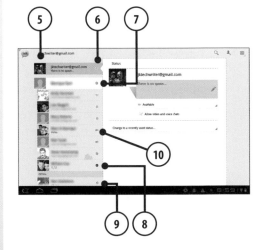

11. Your status is visible to the right of the contact list.

12. You can type in a personal statement (silly or otherwise) in the personal status box.

13. Tap the status drop-down menu and select a status for yourself. Options include Available, Busy, Invisible, and Sign Out.

14. Uncheck the box to disable video and voice-chat capabilities, leaving only text chat.

15. Tap the Recent Status drop-down menu and select an available status.

16. Tap the Invite button.

17. Enter the email address of a friend you want to invite to chat. (It does not have to be a gmail.com address, but only Google users can use video chat. All others are limited to text.) An email is sent to the invitee with a link to click to join a chat or download the Talk app if it's not already installed on his computer, Xoom, or another device.

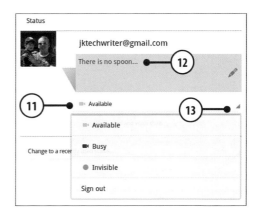

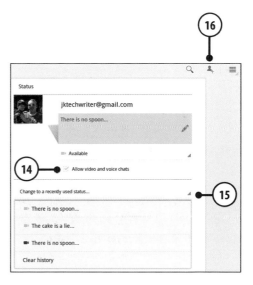

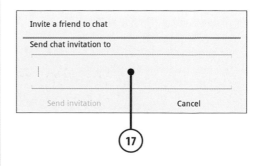

Respect the Status

The user status icon and color assist you to determine when a contact is available for a chat. If the color is red, orange, or gray, don't issue a chat request. Make it a habit to only attempt communication with users who have green icons next to their names.

Using the Webcam for Video Chat

One of the most fun ways to use your Xoom and the Google Talk app is to have a webcam chat. If you have a 3G/4G or Wi-Fi connection, you can use your Xoom to have a webcam chat with friends, co-workers, and anyone else who has a webcam and runs the Talk app. (I frequently use Google Talk and my Xoom's webcam to talk with friends on the other side of the world!) One of the best parts about using the Talk app for a webcam chat is that it's 100% free—no long-distance charges.

1. Open the Talk app and log in with your Google user account.

2. Make sure that there is a check-mark in the Allow Video and Voice Chats checkbox.

3. Scroll down your list of contacts and locate a user with a green video-camera icon next to his name.

4. Tap that person's name.

Instant Message Just to Be Sure

Even if your contact has a green video-camera icon next to his or her name, that doesn't always mean they're ready and available for a call; sometimes, contacts forget to change their status from Available to Busy. When in doubt, type a quick message like, "Are you available for a webchat?" to verify that the contact is available.

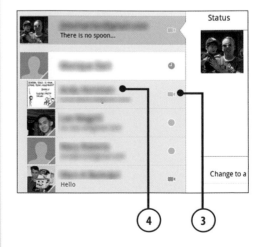

5. The text chat (Instant Messaging) window opens.

6. Type a quick text message just to verify that your contact is in front of his computer (or Xoom) and ready for a webcam chat.

7. If the response is positive, tap the video-camera icon.

8. The webcam chat connection is attempted.

9. Tap the X to cancel the connection attempt. When the connection is made, two different windows appear on the screen.

10. The larger image is the video from your contact's webcam.

11. The smaller image is the video from your webcam—what your contact sees on his screen.

12. Tap the X to close the webcam chat.

13. Sensitivity of the webcam can be controlled by dragging the sensitivity bar left or right.

14. Rotate the Xoom 90 degrees.

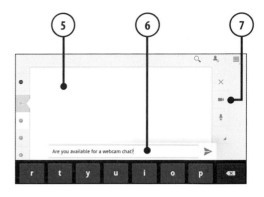

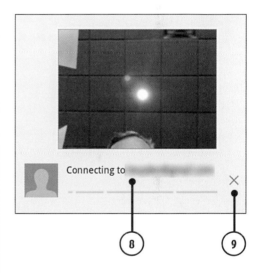

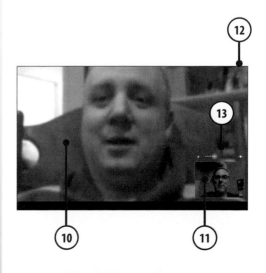

Sensitivity Defined

While using the Xoom's webcam, you're likely holding the Xoom with one or both hands. Even if you think you're holding the Xoom steady, small movements left, right, up, or down are sent by the webcam to your contact and can cause the image your contact sees to be shaky. If that is the case, drag the sensitivity bar to the right a bit or all the way. This forces the webcam to attempt to keep your face in the center of the screen, even with large movements of the Xoom (why you're making a webcam chat call on a roller coaster is your business—just hold on tight). You'll have to experiment to find the best setting.

15. The webcam adjusts the image displayed onscreen.

16. Tap the contact's image and a menu bar appears.

17. Tap to open a text chat window with the contact.

18. Tap to mute the microphone.

19. Tap to toggle back and forth between the front-facing webcam on your Xoom to the rear-facing camera. (This is useful when you want to show your contact your surroundings—maybe a nice view or another family member in the room—and don't want to flip the Xoom around.)

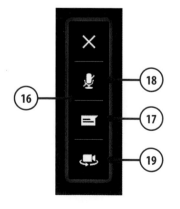

20. If you open the text chat window, you can enter text instead of talking.

21. Tap the video-camera icon to return to the video chat.

22. The mic is muted; tap again to unmute it.

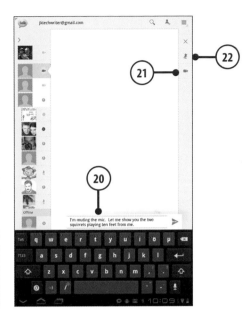

It's Not All Good

WATCH YOUR DATA USAGE

The webcam chat function is fun and useful, but keep in mind that it's sending and receiving a lot of data—both video and sound. If you do not have an unlimited 3G/4G data plan, you might find yourself in for a huge shock when your bill comes. I try to only use the webcam chat feature while on Wi-Fi—then, I don't have to worry about going over my data usage quota.

Instant Message with a Friend

The Google Talk app is also useful for simple text chatting…also known as Instant Messaging. It's not always convenient (or even useful) to have a webcam chat; sometimes it's simply easier to type out a short discussion with a contact. Text chats also use less bandwidth so there's less worry about using up your data usage quota.

1. Open the Talk app.

2. Verify your contact is online and possibly available for a text chat. (A green dot or a green video-camera icon is a good indicator.)

3. Tap the name of the contact.

4. A text chat window opens.

5. Confirm your contact is there with a quick question.

6. Tap the Submit button to send your question. (You can also simply tap the Enter/Return button on the keyboard to also send your text.)

7. If your recipient is at a computer with Talk installed, she sees a pop-up box.

8. Your contact enters a response (and presses Enter when done or taps the Submit button).

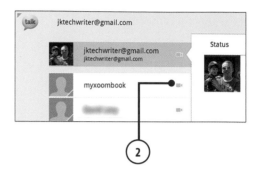

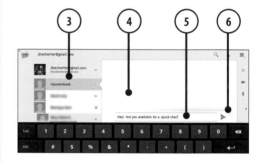

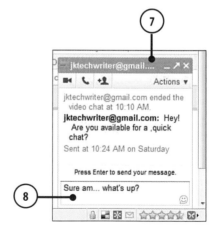

9. You see the response on Xoom's screen.

10. Type another message.

11. Tap the Submit button to send.

12. As the conversation continues, older messages scroll off the screen.

13. If you want to use a microphone and switch from text to voice (not video), tap the microphone button.

14. If you attempt to use the microphone, your contact can click Answer to switch to voice chat.

15. Your contact can click Ignore to stay in text chat mode, and you receive a message indicating that the call was not accepted.

Not Everyone Uses Google Talk

Not everyone has a Google user account, and not everyone wants one. For that reason, you might find yourself having to install an additional chat app to communicate with other friends, family, and colleagues. It's a minor nuisance to endure for the ability to have real-time voice, video, and text conversations with all of your contacts around the world. If a contact isn't using Google Talk for Instant Messaging, it's likely that you can find a chat app in the Android Market that enables you to chat with that person.

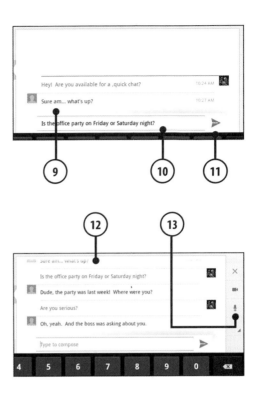

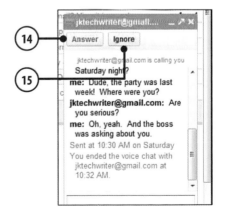

16. To invite another friend into the text chat, tap the chat menu button.

17. Tap the Add to Chat button.

18. Select a contact from the list, and a connection is attempted.

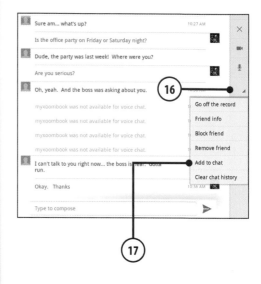

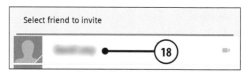

Making a Phone Call with Skype

You already saw how to conduct video, voice, and text chats using Google Talk. But, did you know that you can also use your Xoom to make standard phone calls? By using Skype, which is a free app, you can dial in a phone number and make a call. (Call charges apply, but they're inexpensive.)

1. Open the Android Market and search for Skype.

2. Tap the Skype app to open its information page and download the app.

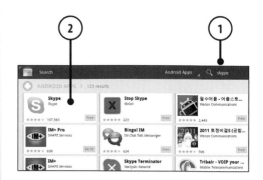

3. After installing the app, open it from the Apps folder.

4. When Skype opens, tap the Continue button.

5. Tap the Create an Account button to create a Skype account if you don't already have one. Follow the instructions and return to the Skype login screen when done.

6. Enter your Skype name and password.

7. Leave the Sign in Automatically box checked to have Skype remember your name and password.

8. Tap the Sign In button to sign into Skype.

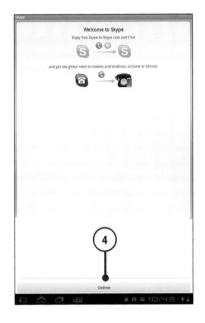

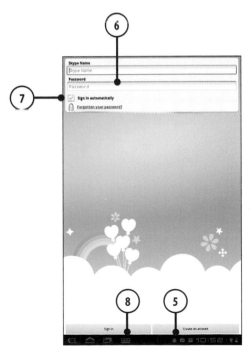

9. Tap the Accept button to acknowledge that Skype cannot be used to make emergency calls (such as the 911 system in the U.S.).

10. Continue to tap the Continue button to take the Skype tour and learn the many features that the app offers.

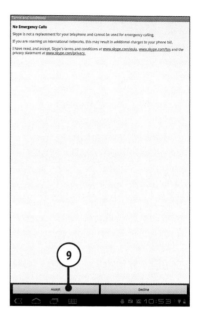

11. Tap the Finish button.

12. Tap the Sync All button if you want your Xoom's contact list to be merged with the Skype list.

13. Tap the Sync with Existing Contacts to add your Skype contacts to your Xoom's contact list.

14. Tap the Don't Sync button to keep your Skype contacts separate from your other contacts (such as your Google email contacts). I used this option.

15. Tap the Continue button.

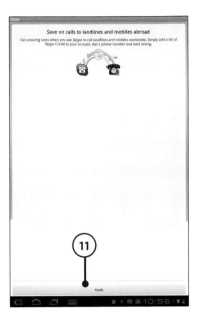

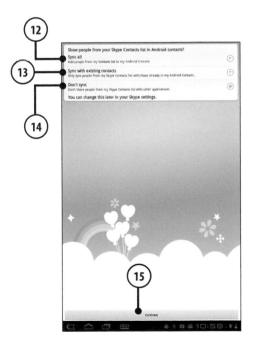

16. You can tap a contact in the Contacts list to make a Skype-to-Skype voice call; it's free, but requires that the other contact have the Skype app installed on a device.

17. Tap the My Info button.

18. Before you can make a phone call with Skype, make sure that you have some Skype credit.

19. If credit exists, tap the Call button.

Add Skype Credit

Before you can make a phone call with Skype on your Xoom, you must add some funds to your Skype account. Visit www.skype.com and log in with your new Skype account. Then, tap the Add Credit button and follow the instructions to use a credit card to add credit to your Skype account. The minimum amount you can add in the U.S. is $10.

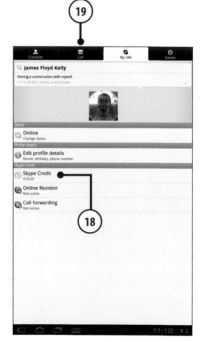

20. Use the dialpad to dial the phone number. (Yes, that's a huge dialpad!)

21. Tap the Call button.

22. A connection is attempted. Make sure that you turn up the volume on your Xoom!

Convert Your Friends!

If you want to avoid fees when making Skype calls, about the only available option is to convince your non-Skype friends to download and install the app (it's available for just about everything—mobile phone, tablets, computers, and more). It's a free app, so with an account, you can talk free to anyone, anywhere in the world.

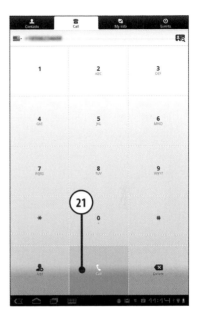

23. The connection is made. Speak as if you are talking on a real phone.

24. The call charge rate is displayed. (I'm calling a U.S. phone number, so I'm being charged $.02 per minute. For a $10 Skype credit, that gives me 500 minutes of talk time…just over 8 hours.)

25. Tap the End Call button to hang up.

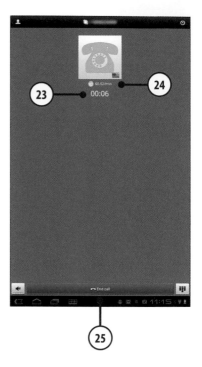

The Xoom is designed to take advantage of many of Google's free services beyond simple email and search engine tools.

In this chapter, you learn about all the free services that Google offers, and see how many of them work great on the Xoom. You learn how to create a family calendar, create a simple website, find the best price on products, and more.

12

Google Galore

Google isn't just a search engine—the company has shaken up the computer-software industry by providing dozens of free, high-quality applications that all run within a web browser.

Although not every Google service works perfectly on your Xoom, it seems that Google is improving its record every day. New services appear almost monthly—sometimes faster— and Google continues to improve its apps so that they will run on just about every platform imaginable, including the Xoom.

Using iGoogle as Your Homepage

In Chapter 4, "Browsing the Web," you learned how to set the homepage for the Browser app. You can obviously set your homepage to anything you like, but Google offers an interesting alternative called iGoogle. It's a customizable webpage that enables you to select and display data from other Google services, such as Gmail, Google Finance, and more.

1. Open the Browser app and visit www.google.com.

2. Tap the More link.

3. Select the Even More option. Every Google service and product is listed here.

4. Scroll down the page to view additional services.

5. Tap the iGoogle service.

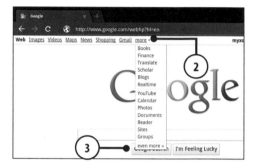

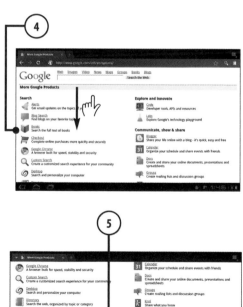

6. The iGoogle webpage appears. Notice that your Google user account is displayed if you are logged in. (If you are not logged in, you must do so before configuring your iGoogle webpage.)

7. Scroll down the page to see that iGoogle has already added some customizable features.

8. The date and time are displayed.

9. You can provide your ZIP code for your local weather forecast.

10. The first five messages in your Gmail Inbox are displayed.

11. The top news story is displayed; a single tap opens the item for more details.

12. Scroll back to the top of the iGoogle page.

13. Place a checkmark in any of the interest boxes that you want to follow. News and video related to these topics are cycled on the iGoogle webpage.

14. Select a background theme that should appear as wallpaper on the iGoogle webpage.

15. Specify your country/region and city/ZIP code for content that is relevant to your location.

16. Tap the See Your Page button to see a preview of your iGoogle webpage.

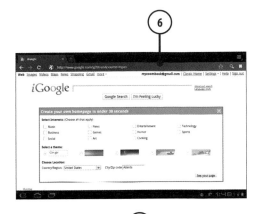

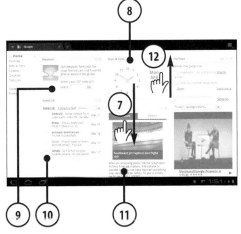

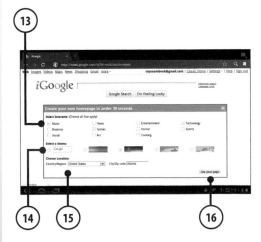

Not All Features May Work Properly

It seems that almost everything Google is developing is in continual testing stages. That's not necessarily a bad thing, because Google is always making improvements and adding features. Just keep in mind that some services that Google offers might be buggy on your Xoom…or might not work at all.

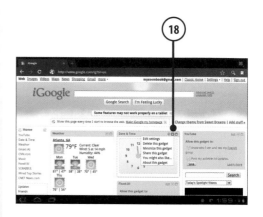

17. iGoogle adds your selected custom features (called gadgets) to the existing ones. This means that you likely need to scroll down the page to view all of your gadgets.

18. To remove an item (such as the Date and Time), tap the small triangle in the upper-right corner of its box and select the Delete This Gadget option.

19. Tap the OK button to confirm the request to delete the gadget.

20. The gadget is removed, and the remaining gadgets are shifted on screen.

21. The Make iGoogle My Homepage link to set the iGoogle webpage as the homepage does not work for the Browser app. You need to set it as your homepage manually; refer to Chapter 4 for the steps.

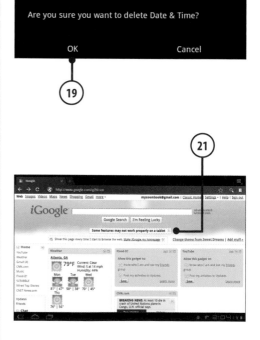

More iGoogle Customization

The Browser app limits you on some configurable items. For example, you can change the placement and order of the various gadgets on the screen, but this can only be done from certain browsers that are commonly found on computers and laptops. This is simply a limitation of the Browser app to support certain tasks; open up a browser on a computer or laptop, log in to your Google user account, and play around with the iGoogle setup; most of the changes you make there are reflected in the iGoogle page stored on your Xoom.

Creating a Free Website

If you've never created a website before and want to, Google Sites is a simple-to-use, free service for creating basic webpages. Don't look for anything fancy—text and some color choices are about it—but for putting together a quick website, it'll do in a pinch.

1. Open the Browser app and visit www.google.com.

2. Tap the More link.

3. Select the Even More option.

4. Scroll down the page to view additional services. Tap the Sites service.

Chapter 12

5. Tap the Create Site button.

6. Google offers templates with color schemes and layouts already pre-configured. Select one or leave the Blank Template option selected.

7. Give your site a name.

8. Scroll down the page.

9. Tap the + sign next to More Options to open it.

10. You can specify whether to make the webpage private or viewable by the world. (If you choose the private option, you have to provide the email addresses of those individuals who should have access.)

11. Enter the code to prove you're human.

12. Tap the Create Site button to create your homepage.

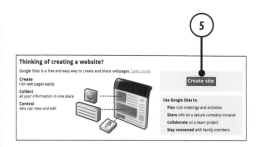

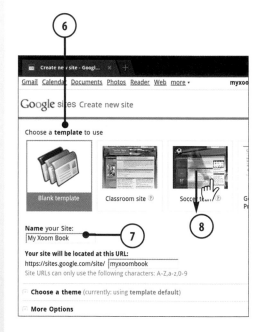

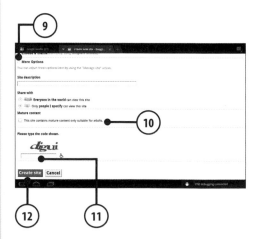

13. Tap the More Actions button to access the drop-down menu; it offers you the ability to print the page, set it as a template, and more.

14. Tap the Create Page button to add a new webpage to your site.

15. Tap the Edit Page button to add text, pictures, and other content. (I choose this option.)

16. Each section of the webpage has a border box. Tap inside an empty box to select it and add text, images, and more.

17. Tap inside the box that includes content to edit that content.

18. Tap a menu (Insert, Format, Table, or Layout) for additional features and tasks. (Not all the tasks found in these menus are supported by the Browser app.)

19. Tap the Link option to add a web address/URL.

20. Use the formatting buttons on your text.

21. Tap the Save button when you're done.

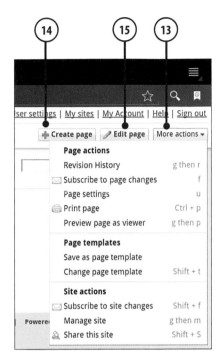

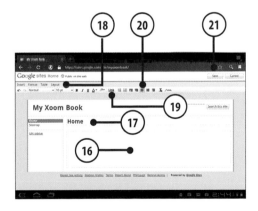

22. The homepage is created, and text and links are visible.

23. Notice the web page address in the address bar; it follows a format of sites.google.com/ yoursitename. This is the address you can share with the world or email to your friends and family.

Sites Have Much More to Offer

Entire chapters can be written on using the Sites service. I only show you how to create a simple website with one page, but you can create some complex websites using Sites. Explore the Help menu to learn about every feature that Sites offers. Keep in mind that Sites is free—it's a perfect solution for creating quick websites for garage sales, a soccer team, a classroom project, and more.

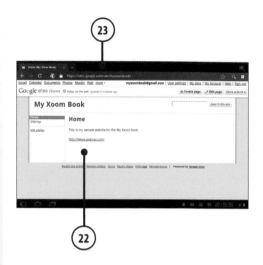

Finding the Lowest Price

Most everyone is familiar with Google, but not many people know about its excellent product review and pricing service, called Google Product Search (formerly called Froogle). With Google Product Search, you can search for items you're considering purchasing and find local and online businesses that sell it. Best of all, you can organize your search results by price, which enables you to quickly find the best deal.

1. Open the Browser app and visit www.google.com.

2. Tap the More link.

3. Select the Even More option.

4. Scroll down the page and tap the Product Search service.

5. The Product Search service works just like the Google search tool. Type in what you're looking for—product name, ISBN (for books), or even a UPC code.

6. Tap the Search button when you're done.

7. Products matching your search criteria are listed.

8. Tap the Sort By menu.

Using Google Product Searching for Haggling

Your Xoom is portable, so take advantage of that and take it with you when you go shopping. If you find an item at a local store for $39.95, run the name of the item through Google's Product Search and see whether you can find it cheaper. If it's offered by an online store for $34.95, that might sound like a deal, but always remember to check shipping costs. You might find that the item costs $7.50 to ship, which no longer makes it a deal. If you really do find a substantial savings either online or at a nearby competitor, don't hesitate to ask for a manager and show her the savings you can get by waiting a few days or more for the item to be shipped or spending 10 minutes and a little gasoline driving down the road to a competitor. You might find the manager willing to negotiate.

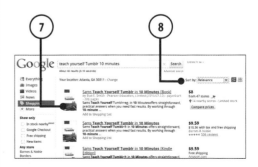

9. Select the Price: Low to High option.

10. The product listing is reordered based on price, lowest to highest.

11. Tap the seller name to view more information and place an order (if it's an online shop).

12. Use the filter checkboxes to limit the results; options include showing only those sellers near your location, only sellers who use Google Checkout, and sellers offering free shipping.

Using Price-Comparison Apps

A number of apps have appeared on the Android Market that enable you to use the Xoom's camera to take a photo of a product's UPC (barcode). The app then identifies the product and attempts to find the best prices at both local shops in your area and online stores. Search the Android Market for Barcode Scanner and you'll find the most popular scanning apps. (Interestingly enough, one of the most popular apps of this type is called… Barcode Scanner.

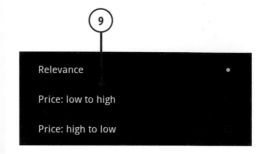

Relevance

Price: low to high

Price: high to low

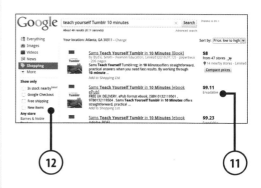

Creating a Family Calendar

Google offers you the ability to create a calendar that can be shared by multiple people—family members, co-workers, and sports team members are all good examples. Having a shared calendar enables the participants to track things such as doctor appointments, school breaks, vacation days, and more.

1. Open the Browser app and visit www.google.com.

2. Tap the More link.

3. Select the Even More option.

4. Scroll down the page to view additional services.

5. Tap the Calendar service.

6. The calendar you automatically get when you create a Google account opens. It's linked to your email address.

7. Tap the Add button to add a new calendar.

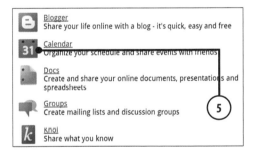

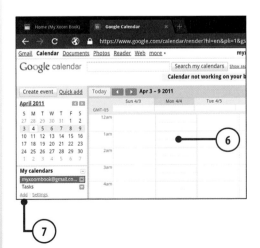

8. Give the calendar a name and provide other requested information, such as time zone.

9. Scroll down the page.

10. Do not place a checkmark in the Make This Calendar Public checkbox.

11. Enter the email address for each person who should have access to your shared calendar.

12. Tap the small triangle to allow a person to edit the calendar (recommended for shared calendars).

13. Select the Make Changes to Events option to allow someone to add his own events or edit existing events.

14. Select the See All Event Details option to allow someone to only view the calendar.

15. After providing a person's email address and configuring the permission settings, tap the Add Person button.

16. Repeat this process for each person you want to provide access to your shared calendar.

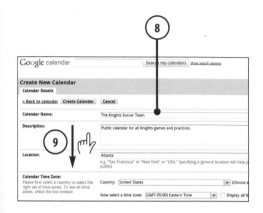

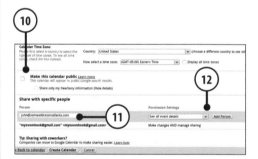

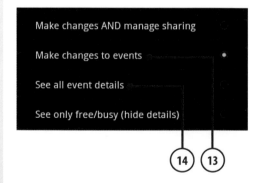

17. Tap the trashcan icon to remove someone and prevent him from viewing the calendar.

18. Tap the small triangle to modify a user's permission settings in the drop-down menu.

19. After all shared calendar members are added, scroll to the bottom of the screen.

20. Tap the Create Calendar button.

21. The new calendar appears.

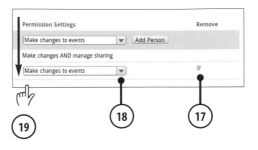

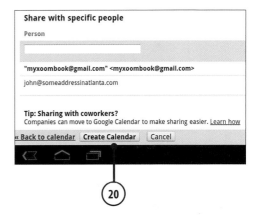

22. Tap inside the calendar on a day or time to create a new event.

23. Enter the event name and time.

24. Select the new calendar from the drop-down menu.

25. Tap the Create Event button.

26. The event is added—the color of the text matches the color assigned to the new calendar.

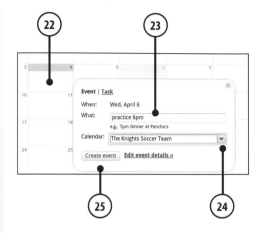

Shared Calendar Usage

Those individuals whose email addresses you provided when setting up the calendar receive an email with a link that enables them to access the shared calendar—they can do this even if they do not have a Google user account. Users who have the ability to modify events can add events to the calendar (a family could use this to let the soccer team know when they'll be out of town) or modify events (such as changing a game time due to bad weather).

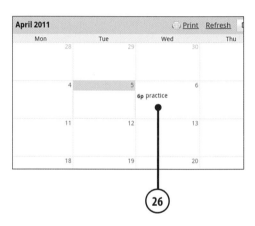

Email Alerts for Topics of Interest

If you have topics that interest you (sports, music, technology, politics, and so on), Google can provide you with up-to-date alerts when news related to your interests appears on blogs, online news sources, in a video, or discussion forums. It doesn't matter if it's a hobby, a sports team, a politician, or even a broader search term (such as cars). If you want to receive emails from Google when new content appears related to your interests, you'll enjoy the Google Alerts service.

1. Open the Browser app and visit www.google.com.

2. Tap the More link.

3. Select the Even More option.

4. Scroll down the page to view additional services.

5. Tap the Alerts service.

6. Enter the search topic for which you want to receive alerts. (I select Arduino, an electronics device used by hobbyists.)

7. Use the Type drop-down menu to select a source for results. The options include five basic sources—News, Blogs, Realtime, Video, Discussions—and Everything searches all five sources.

8. Select a time period to perform the search. Options include: As It Happens, Once a Day, and Once a Week.

9. The Volume setting has two options: Only the Best Results and All Results.

10. Provide an email address in the Deliver To field or select Feed if you use an RSS Reader (see the next section for more details).

11. Click the Create Alert button to start the process and check your email (or an RSS reader, such as Google Reader) for a compilation of all the results related to your search term.

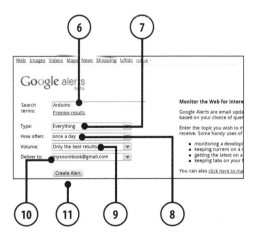

It's Not All Good

INFORMATION OVERLOAD

If you like Google Alerts, you'll definitely find yourself fine-tuning your alert settings over time as you attempt to refine the search and reduce unwanted alerts while increasing the results that interest you. That's why it's best to be specific with your search term (versus using broad topics such as cars or U.S. Senate). With specific search requests, you're less likely to be overwhelmed with results and more likely to find exactly what you need. There is always a Manage Your Alerts link on the Alerts page that enables you to edit your existing Google Alert searches. It's always best to start with settings that cause the fewest interruptions in your day and take the least amount of time to sift through, so consider using Only the Best Results and Once a Week for alert settings and then modify if you find you need more results more often.

Using Google Reader

If you're a fan of reading blogs and other news sources, you might want to consider using an application that pulls the information from your favorite sources into a single location. Blogs and other sources of news and information frequently make their content available using what's called an RSS feed—it's simply a way to deliver the content to an email address or RSS reader. The Xoom is a perfect device to use an RSS reader; it's light, portable, can pull in content via Wi-Fi and 3G/4G, and it has a nice large screen on which to read it all.

1. Open the Browser app and visit www.google.com.

2. Tap the More link.

3. Select the Even More option.

4. Scroll down the page to view additional services.

5. Tap the Reader service.

6. Tap the Add a Subscription button.

Google Reader Advanced

Google Reader has many more features than I can write about, so I encourage you to consult the Help documentation (click the Help link in the upper-right corner of the Google Reader web page). There are tools to help you manage large amounts of information, including options to help you determine what you've read, comments you've posted or are following, and trends of hot topics.

7. Enter the web address of a blog or website. (You can also enter a search term to look for websites, blogs, and other online sources.)

8. Tap the Add button.

9. Repeat steps 7 and 8 to add as many sources of online content as you like.

10. Tap the Back button.

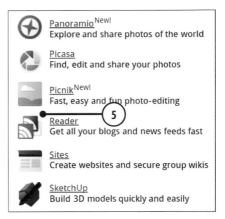

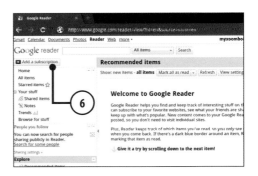

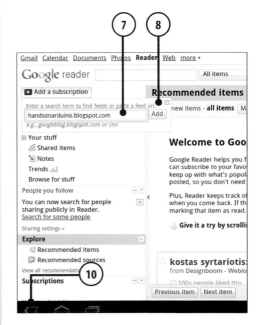

11.   Your subscriptions are listed, with the number of articles, videos, or discussions listed in parentheses.

12.   The total number of unread articles for all subscriptions appears in bold.

13.   Tap a Subscription source to open and view all of its content.

14.   Tap the Refresh button to have Google Reader attempt to contact the sources and pull down new items.

15.   Tap the List button.

16.   Articles are listed by title and are easier to read and search.

17.   Bold titles represent articles you have not yet read.

18.   Non-bold titles indicate articles you have read.

19.   Tap the All Items option.

20.   All subscriptions are visible and the Source is listed in the first column.

21.   Tap Feeds for Google Alerts to open and view any Google Alerts you have configured.

Google Alerts

In the previous section, you learned how to create Google Alerts. Rather than provide your email address for the location to send the results, you can choose to send to a reader, such as Google Reader. Choose the Feed option when selecting the Deliver To option, and the Google Reader is automatically selected.

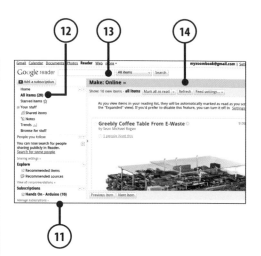

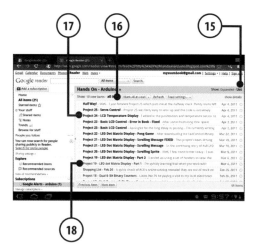

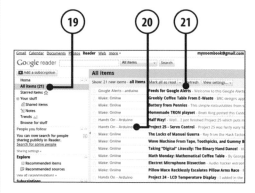

The Xoom is great for playing games, and the touch screen and tilt sensor allow you to control many games without a joystick.

In this chapter, you see just how much fun the Xoom can be when it comes to games. Because of its large screen and dual-core processor, the Xoom is a perfect gaming platform for playing some old favorites... as well as many new games.

13

→ Don't Get Angry (Angry Birds)

→ Slicing Some Fruit (Fruit Ninja)

→ Old School Arcade (Air Attack HD)

→ How's Your Balance? (Steamball)

Games, Games, Games

You might have purchased your Xoom tablet for email or web browsing or other "serious" work, but let's face it—the Xoom has a big color screen and a dual-core processor, which makes it a serious game-playing machine.

It probably comes as no surprise that the Android Market has thousands of available games. Some are free, while others cost a small fee. But rest assured—no matter what kind of games you like to play, there's a game for you in the Market.

Don't Get Angry

The game Angry Birds is a phenomenon! If you haven't heard of it, well...that's a shock, because the game is incredibly popular. What makes it more shocking is its simple premise: Use a slingshot to fling some angry birds toward some pigs that have captured their eggs. The pigs have barricaded themselves in buildings made of wood or ice or concrete, so it's not always easy. Different birds have different powers, and the levels get crazy and complicated the more you play. The game is available from the Android Market for free (with minimal advertising).

1. Open the Android Market.

2. Search for Angry Birds.

3. Tap the game to go to its information page for purchasing and download and installation.

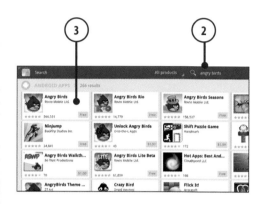

Downloading and Installing Games

Downloading games (free and paid) and installing them is fast and easy. Refer to Chapter 7, "The Android Market," for instructions on purchasing games, downloading, installing, and uninstalling. This chapter assumes that you can search the Android Market for the games mentioned and install and run them from the Apps folder.

4. After Angry Birds loads, tap the Play button.

5. Angry Birds is broken into six stories: Poached Eggs, Mighty Hoax, Danger Above, The Big Setup, Ham 'Em High, and Golden Eggs.

6. Use a swipe gesture to move between stories.

7. A padlock icon means that a story is locked; each story (and its levels) must be solved before you move to the next story.

8. Tap the first story, Poached Eggs. Each story has multiple levels.

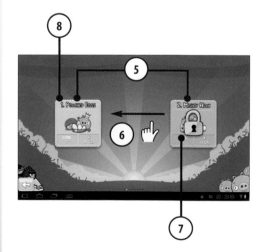

9. Levels that are unlocked and playable are given a number.

10. Levels that are locked have a pad-lock icon.

11. Tap the first level to open it. After a small animation plays, the level begins.

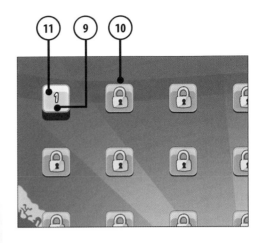

12. Instructions are provided each time you are given a new type of bird to use. View the visual instruction—in this example, you see how to use your finger to tap and hold the red bird. You then pull your finger back to use the slingshot. The pig is the target.

13. Tap the checkmark to view the remaining instruction images.

Cheating at Angry Birds

There are well more than 150 levels in the entire game, and some folks either don't have the time or patience to complete every level. If that's you, you might be happy to know that some enterprising app developers made their own apps that "unlock" all the levels. Search for Angry Birds in the Android Market, and you can find these cheat apps—just don't tell anyone that you used them!

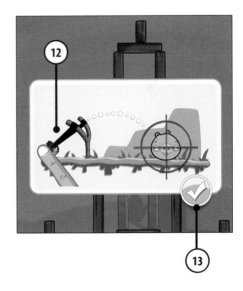

14. When the level starts, the screen zooms in on the birds in the sling-shot. (You get three for the first level.)

15. Use a pinch gesture to zoom out. (Touch the screen with your thumb and pointer finger apart and then bring them together.)

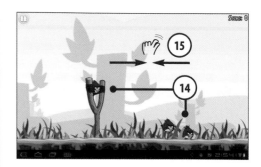

16. The entire level is now visible, including birds, slingshot, and the pig in his castle.

17. Tap and hold the first red bird, pull back the slingshot, and release!

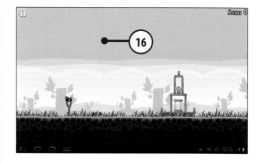

18. Wheeeee!

19. A white line represents the bird's path as it flies toward the pig. This helps you line up your next shot if the first bird doesn't knock down the castle and eliminate the pig.

20. The bird successfully knocks down enough of the castle to hit and eliminate the pig.

Super Birds and Golden Eggs

I don't want to spoil any surprises, but be aware that different types of birds become available as you progress with the game. Most of these birds have a superpower, so be sure to view the instructions when they appear so you know how to properly use a bird. Also, if you find a golden egg in a level somewhere, try to hit the egg with a bird. If you manage to do so, go back to the game's menu and swipe past the last story. There's a Golden Egg story with some fun surprises.

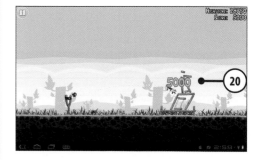

21. Your score is displayed, and stars are awarded based on how few birds it took to win and the level of destruction brought on the evil pigs.

22. Tap to replay the level.

23. Tap to move to the next level.

24. Tap to return to the level screen to view all the unlocked levels.

Slicing Some Fruit

Sometimes, the simplest games are the most addictive. Using only your fingers and a swiping gesture, you become the Swiping Samurai as you unleash your fury on the flying fruit in Fruit Ninja!

1. Search the Android Market for Fruit Ninja THD. It is currently priced at U.S. $3.10. The THD version is optimized for Xoom.

2. Tap the game to view its information screen and purchase and download.

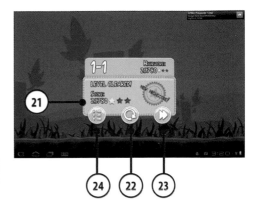

3. Open the game after the installation is complete. When Fruit Ninja opens, you are presented with five options.

4. Swipe with your finger to quit the game. (Taps won't work in Fruit Ninja—everything is done with a swipe of your finger and the onscreen sword.)

5. Swipe with your finger to play a single-player game. (I use this option for the remainder of this section.)

6. Swipe with your finger to play a multiplayer game.

7. Swipe to enter the Dojo where you can select different swords. (They have no effect on game play, but they do have different colors, screen effects, and different wallpapers.)

8. Swipe to log in to the Feint gaming system, which tracks your scores and other players.

9. Swipe for Classic mode—miss three pieces of fruit or slice a bomb and the game ends. (I select this option.)

10. Swipe for Zen mode—no bombs and 90 seconds to slice as many pieces of fruit as possible.

11. Swipe for Arcade mode—60 seconds and points are deducted for every bomb you slice.

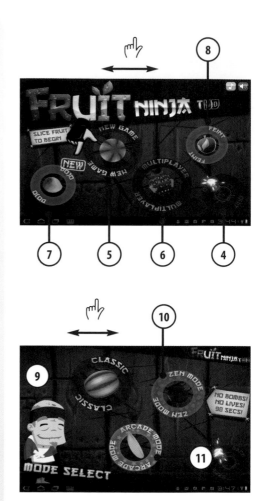

12. When Classic mode starts, fruit begins flying from the bottom of the screen, moving up and then falling down. Swipe a piece of fruit to slice it in half.

13. Don't swipe a bomb, or it's game over.

14. Each red X represents a piece of fruit that dropped off the screen unsliced.

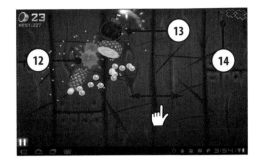

15. Swipe to replay the game.

16. Swipe to quit and return to main menu.

17. Tap to see scores from other players (and how you compare).

18. Multiplayer mode divides the screen, with each player using half the screen. (The multiplayer menu allows you to adjust the speed of the fruit and select a timed or untimed game.)

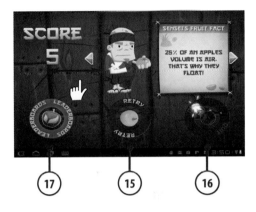

19. Identical fruits and bombs are simultaneously thrown. If a player slices a bomb, he or she loses.

Special Fruit

During a game, you might see some rare bananas fly by. Don't miss them! Slicing a rare banana provides bonus points, slows down the speed of the flying fruit, and more.

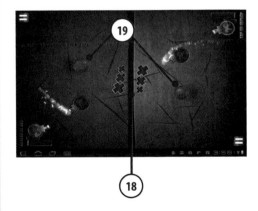

Old School Arcade

If you rotate your Xoom to vertical mode, you can almost see and hear those old 1980s arcade games like Pacman and Space Invaders. Well, plenty of games have that early arcade look and feel and work great in vertical mode. One of my favorites is AirAttack HD. (Part 1 is free; if you like it, you can purchase additional levels with Part 2 at U.S. $1.92.) AirAttack has you at the controls of a WWII fighter; you can use your finger to direct the airplane or configure the game for tilt-control and control the airplane by tilting the Xoom left, right, forward, and back.

1. Search the Android Market for AirAttack HD Part 1.

2. Tap the game to view its information screen and download the game.

3. Open the game after the installation is complete.

4. Tap the Settings button on the main menu to configure the controls.

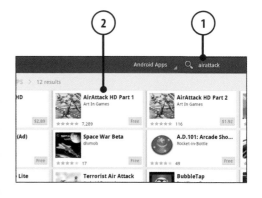

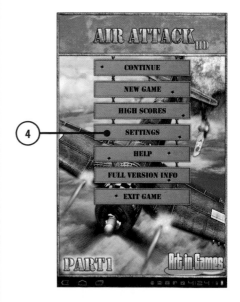

5. Tap the Tilt button if you want to control the plane by tilting the Xoom left, right, forward, or back.

6. Tap the Touch button if you want to place a single finger on the touch screen that controls the plane's movement. (I prefer this method and select it.)

7. Tap the Back button to return to the main menu.

8. Tap the New Game button.

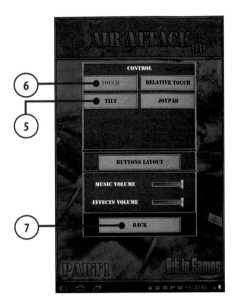

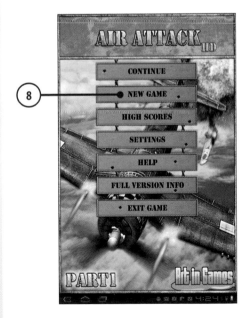

9. Select the difficulty level. (I choose Easy but feel free to choose Medium or Hard if you like a challenge.)

10. Tap the Start button to begin the game.

11. Select your airplane by tapping one of the two options. (They look different onscreen but operate the same.)

12. Read game tips before starting the game.

13. Tap the screen to begin.

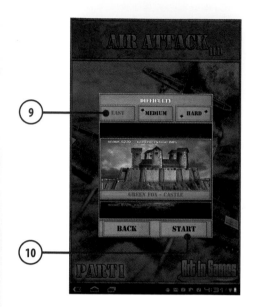

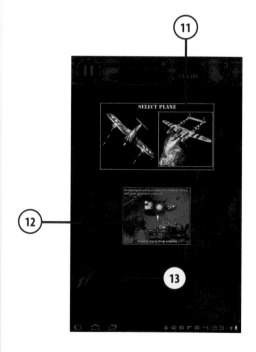

14. Place and drag your finger just behind the airplane. In whatever direction you drag your finger on the screen, the plane follows.

15. Ready status indicates that a bomb is loaded.

16. Double-tap the screen to drop bombs over targets. You must be just below and behind the target (on the screen).

17. Tap the weapon toggle to switch back and forth between bullets and any special weapons you purchased.

18. Dodge enemy airplanes and bullets.

19. Keep an eye on your plane's health bar. When it's gone, your plane drops from the sky.

20. You start with four lives—one on the screen and three in reserve.

21. Tap the Pause button to pause the game. Tap the Resume button to continue the game.

22. After destroying an enemy aircraft, there are often colored coins floating on the screen. Collect them for cash rewards that can be used in the store.

23. When a store appears onscreen (it's a floating castle with a green dotted line surrounding it), drag the plane inside the circle to land and make purchases.

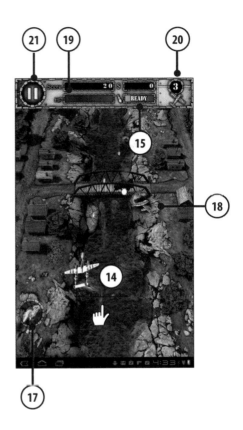

24. The store displays with new weapons available, if you have the cash. Tap an item's button to purchase it.

25. Weapons that have a padlock icon are not available, but they might be available later on if you perform the action described on the button.

Bonuses

Don't ignore the rewards left over after destroying an enemy target. These rewards add cash to your bank account so you can upgrade your weapons and buy special bonus weapons. Also, keep an eye out for the red crosses that add points back to your health meter and keep you going a bit longer!

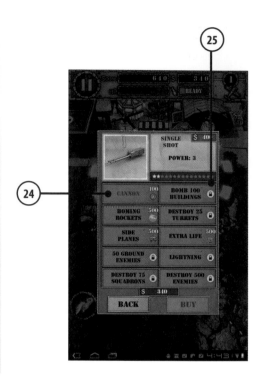

How's Your Balance?

Xoom can detect when you tilt it left and right, forward and backward. And many games take advantage of this feature. One addictive game that requires no tapping on the screen is called Steamball. You can download a free version of it to see if you like it (fewer levels), and the full version runs U.S. $1.40.

1. Search the Android Market for Steamball. You can download either the free version (with limited levels) or purchase the full version.

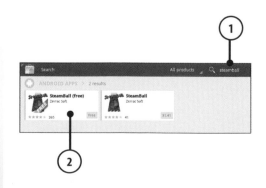

2. Tap the game to view its information screen and either purchase or download a version. (For the free version, levels must be unlocked sequentially; the paid version allows you to play them in any order.)

3. Open the game after the installation is complete.

4. The Steamball main menu opens.

5. Tap New Game.

6. Select a difficulty level by tapping Easy, Normal, or Hard. Each level has a number of mazes from which to select. (I select Normal.)

7. After selecting a difficulty level, tap a maze name to select it. (I select Platforms 2.) The level opens.

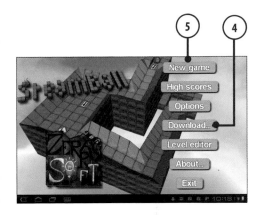

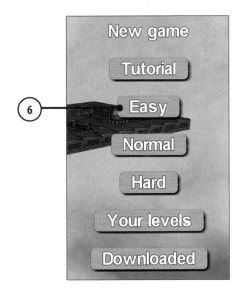

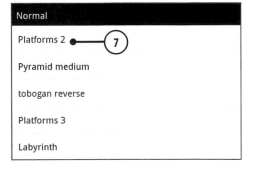

8. Hold the Xoom parallel to the floor as the tilt sensor is calibrated.

9. The timer counts down from 3 and then the game begins.

10. When the game begins, tilt the Xoom left, right, forward and back.

11. If you tilt the Xoom left, the ball rolls to the left on the screen; tilting it to the right causes the ball to roll to the right.

12. Tilting the Xoom forward causes the ball to roll forward; tilting it back causes the ball to roll backward.

Ball Speed

The speed of the ball is controlled by how far you tilt the Xoom in a particular direction—the greater the tilt in a direction, the faster the ball rolls in that same direction.

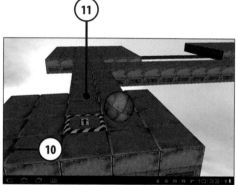

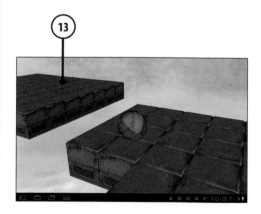

13. Tilt the Xoom so that the ball rolls and stays on the solid surface.

14. Look for the Finish Point to win the game; it is represented by a checkered flag icon. When you get the ball to the checkered flag, the level is complete.

15. Tap the Next Level button to play the next level.

16. Tap the Back to Menu button to return to the main menu.

More Features

In addition to the three difficulty levels and their respective mazes, you can also download levels created by other users and design your own. Use the Level Editor button on the main menu to design your own levels and upload them for other Steamball fans. Use the Download button to find levels from other owners. You can then access your own levels and any downloaded levels by selecting New Game and choosing either Your Levels or Downloaded, respectively.

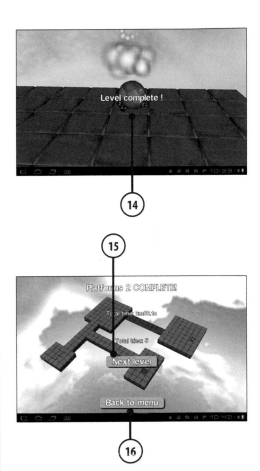

Your Xoom becomes a personal assistant with the right choice of productivity apps.

In this chapter, you learn about some great apps that can make your life more productive. The portability of Xoom makes it a great little personal assistant with the right apps…and this chapter introduces you to a handful of them.

14

→ Files on the Go (Dropbox)
→ Personal To Do List (Taskos To Do List)
→ Keeping the Family Organized (Cozi Family Organizer Premium)
→ Password/Account Management (SafeWallet)

Be Productive

Our work and personal lives can be hectic at times. With our on-the-go lifestyles, we have so much information to manage, phone numbers to remember, appointments to attend, grocery shopping to do, and more.

With the Xoom's portability and good battery life, you'll want to investigate the available apps that can help you with your daily activities. The Xoom can be a great assistant—if you let it. Adding a little organization to your life via the Xoom is a great way to increase your personal productivity and maybe free up some more time in your busy day.

Files on the Go

If you have a computer or laptop (at home, in the office, or both), at one time or another, you have probably found yourself wishing you could access a certain file while not sitting in front of that device. With a little configuration and planning on your part, the Xoom can easily get to files that you choose to make available. All that's required is installing a free app on your Xoom called Dropbox and a matching app on the computer or laptop and creating a user account. You get two gigabytes (GB) of free storage space to start with and can purchase more later if you find yourself running out of room.

1. Open the Android Market.

2. Search for Dropbox.

3. Click the app to go to its information page for purchasing and download and installation.

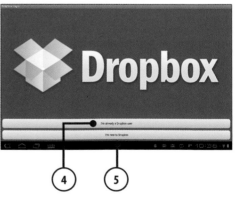

Downloading and Installing Apps

Jump back to Chapter 7, "The Android Market," for instructions on purchasing apps, downloading, installing, and uninstalling them. This chapter assumes that you can search the Android Market for the apps mentioned and install and run them from the Apps folder.

---

4. After Dropbox installs, tap I'm Already a Dropbox User if you have a Dropbox user account. (I use this option because I already created an account and installed the app on my home laptop.)

5. Tap I'm New to Dropbox to create a user account if you don't already have a Dropbox user account. Follow the instructions and remember the password you created.

Install Dropbox on a Home or Work PC or Laptop

You also need to open a web browser to www.dropbox.com and download and install the Dropbox application on a home or work computer. The application puts a Dropbox icon on the desktop. Double-click the icon, log in with your Dropbox user account, and drag and drop (or copy and paste) files from your computer to the Dropbox folder. After files are loaded into the Dropbox folder, the work or home computer does not need to be turned on. The Dropbox network securely synchronizes any files placed in a Dropbox (whether that file was added on a computer, a mobile phone, or even your Xoom) and "pushes" it out to all other Dropbox devices. This enables you to access any files stored in your Dropbox folder from multiple devices, no matter if the other devices are disabled or turned off.

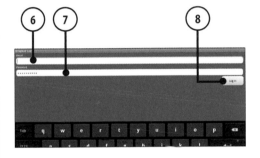

6. Enter your email address that serves as your Dropbox username.

7. Enter your Dropbox password.

8. Tap the Log In button. After you log in to Dropbox, all files and folders are displayed.

9. Tap a folder to open and view any files stored in it.

10. Tap a document to open it.

11. Use a swipe gesture to scroll down the screen to view more files and folders.

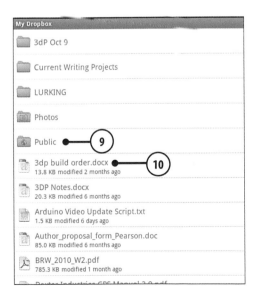

Opening Files in Dropbox

The Dropbox app is capable of opening many different file types, including PDF, DOC/DOCX, JPG, and more. However, you might have to use the Android Market to find apps that are capable of opening other file types should Dropbox inform you that it is unable to display a file.

12. Tap the Menu button.

13. Tap the Refresh button to refresh the Dropbox folder; this is useful if you just added a file to Dropbox on your work or home computer and the file has not been synchronized with the Dropbox network.

14. Tap the New button to create a folder or a new text file (for creating a quick note). Other options include picture and video (both of which open the Camera app).

15. Tap the Upload button to select and copy a picture, video, or MP3 file stored on your Xoom and place it in the Dropbox folder.

16. Tap the Help button to learn about additional Dropbox features.

17. Tap the Settings button.

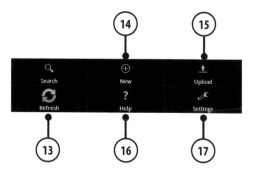

18. View the total storage space in your Dropbox account and the percentage used.

19. Tap Unlink Device from Dropbox to break the connection with your Dropbox account. Files stored and associated with your Dropbox account are no longer available.

20. Use the About section to watch a video that demonstrates how to use Dropbox, send an email to friends to invite them to use Dropbox (you get more free storage space added if a friend accepts), and send feedback or questions to the Dropbox development team.

21. The advanced features are troubleshooting tools that are used by the Dropbox development team should you contact them with a technical problem you encounter.

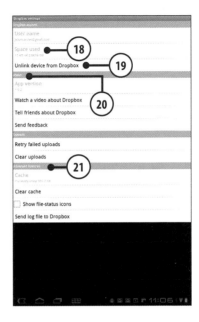

Access Dropbox Anywhere

Dropbox apps exist for the Xoom and other tablets as well as mobile phones and Windows, Mac, and Linux computers. Just log in to www.dropbox.com, and you can view your Dropbox folder from any device that has an Internet connection and a web browser installed.

Personal To Do List

A lot of people use To Do lists—there's something about those unchecked boxes next to each item that just drives people crazy. If you're a fan of To Do lists and want to add that functionality to your Xoom, you will love Taskos. Taskos is an extremely simple, no-frills To Do list app that has everything you need.

1. Search the Android Market for the free app Taskos.

2. Tap the app to view its information screen and purchase and download. Return to the Xoom's home screen after Taskos is installed.

3. Tap and hold on an empty spot on the display.

4. Tap the Widgets option.

5. Scroll through the list (left and right) and tap the Taskos BIG (4×4) option.

6. The Taskos widget is added to your primary home screen.

7. After adding the Taskos widget, tap the Home button.

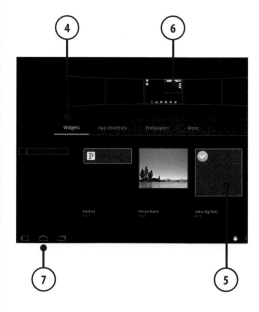

8. The Taskos widget appears—tap and hold it to drag and relocate it to a new location or another home screen.

9. Create your first To Do item by tapping in the text field.

10. Use the onscreen keyboard to enter a task.

11. Tap the Add button to add it to your To Do list. (I choose this option.)

12. Tap the Cancel button to return to the home screen.

13. Your new item appears in the list.

14. Tap the Microphone icon to add an item by speaking.

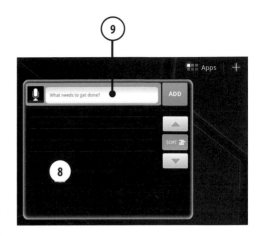

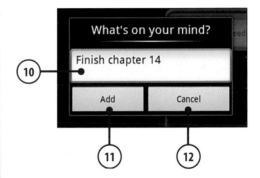

15. When the Speak Now pop-up appears, speak clearly. (I say, "Finish Chapter 15.")

16. Taskos attempts to translate your words into text.

17. Tap Say Again if the translation was not correct and you want to speak again.

18. Tap the Add button if the translation was correct. (I choose this option.)

19. Tap any item in your To Do list. The Task Management screen opens.

20. Tap an item you want to edit or for which you want to set a due date. The Task Edit menu displays.

21. Tap the Priority button for High, Normal, or Low priority.

22. High priority items have a red band to the left of their name, Normal items have a yellow band, and Low items have a green band.

23. Tap the Category button to select General, Work, or Home.

24. Work and Home items will have their category name displayed below the item description.

25. Tap the Date button to set a specific due date for the item.

26. The due date appears below the item's description.

27. Tap the Share button to send the item's text via email.

28. Tap the More button to add a note. (Use the onscreen keyboard to provide more details if needed—these notes do not appear on the To Do list.)

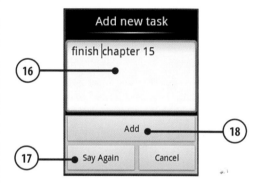

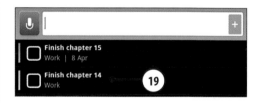

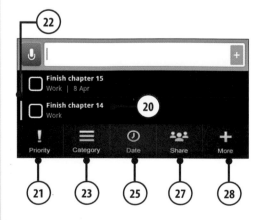

It's Not All Good

NO CALENDAR INTEGRATION

Right now, there is no synchronization between Taskos and a calendar app, such as Google Calendar. That would be helpful for those times when you're online (using a home or work computer) and don't have your Xoom handy. Right now, the Share button lists Dropbox (if you are using it), but if you attempt to upload your Taskos To Do list via Dropbox, you get a message telling you that the feature hasn't yet been implemented. That's good news and bad news—good news that it might be a new feature added soon and bad news that there doesn't appear (yet) to be a way to make your Taskos To Do list items visible on other devices or computers.

Keeping the Family Organized

If you have a family, you have a lot of things to track—doctor appointments, oil changes, school activities, grocery lists, and much more. You were already introduced to Taskos in the previous section, but if you have more than one person to keep track of (kids count double!), you might want to check out Cozi Family Organizer, which is a great app with some cool features for moms, dads, kids, and even the pet. (Your dog isn't going to drive himself to the vet!)

1. Search the Android Market for Cozi Family Organizer Premium. The premium version is U.S. $5.99—the free version has a small box that displays advertisements and isn't annoying, so feel free to try out the free version first.

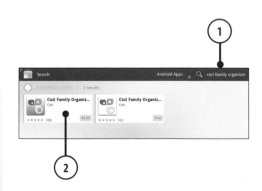

2. Tap the app to view its information screen and to download the app. Open Cozi Family Organizer after installation is complete.

3. If you don't already have a Cozi account, tap the Sign Up button and follow the instructions. (If more than one person in your family will use Cozi, make sure to specify a family name and password during the sign-up process.)

4. After you log in to Cozi, the Cozi Family Organizer main menu screen appears. Before using the app, you should add additional family members and give them access to the shared family tools (Calendar, To Do List, Shopping List, and Journal).

5. Tap the Settings button.

6. Your account is displayed, along with a colored dot that is associated with your name. (Mine is blue.)

7. Tap the Add Adult 2 button to add another family member.

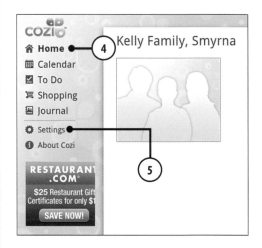

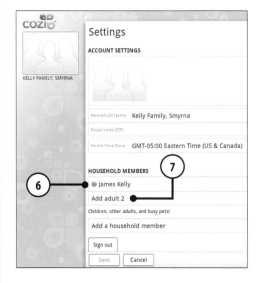

8. Enter the name of another family member.

9. Tap the Color button to assign a different color.

10. Tap the Save button to add the family member.

11. Tap Add a Household Member to add additional names.

12. Tap the Save button to return to the Cozi main menu screen.

13. After adding additional family members, tap the To Do button.

14. Tap in the text box and type a To Do item.

15. Tap the Enter button when you're done.

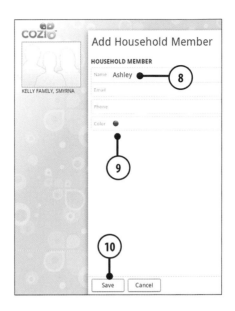

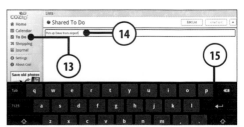

16. Tap the Lists button.

17. Select the To Do list for another family member.

18. Add a To Do item for another family member in the text box; tap Enter when done.

19. Tap the Shopping button.

20. Tap the Create a New Shopping List button.

21. Enter the name of the new list.

22. Tap the Done button.

23. Tap the Save button.

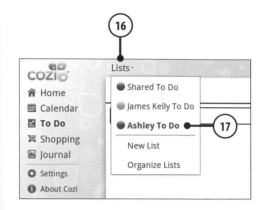

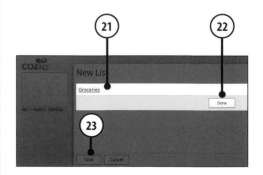

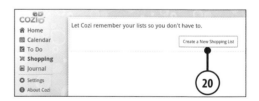

24. Add items to your list (groceries, in this example). The list automatically saves, and you can leave and return to it anytime by tapping the Shopping button.

25. Tap the Lists button to create and name a new list.

26. Tap the checkbox next to an item to place a checkmark to indicate an item has been purchased (or a task completed).

27. Tap the Calendar button.

28. Tap to add an entry for a specific day and time.

29. Tap the left arrow to view the previous month.

30. Tap the right arrow to view the next month.

31. Tap to switch to Month View.

32. Tap the Journal button.

33. Tap the Jot Down a Moment button.

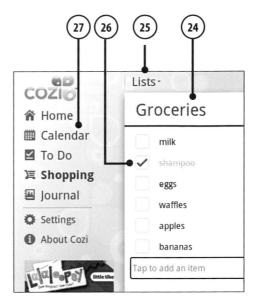

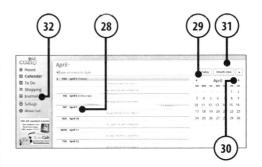

34. Enter a description or short note in the text box.

35. Tap the date box if you want to add the time to the entry.

36. Tap the Add a Photo button to view the Gallery and select a photo to associate, or launch the Camera app to take a photo.

37. Tap the Save button.

38. Journal entries are visible to all family members using Cozi. Journal entries are a great way for family members to share what they're doing, places they've visited, and other information.

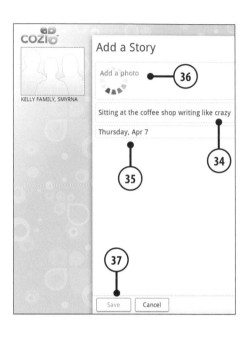

Calendar, Shopping, and Journal

The Calendar, Shopping, and Journal tools are always shared between family members using Cozi. The To Do tool is the only tool with which you can specify a family member and provide unique To Do items. (Sorry to husbands out there whose wives run Cozi.)

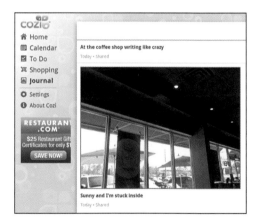

Password/Account Management

In this chapter alone, if you installed Dropbox and Cozi, you also added two new usernames and passwords to remember. Security experts tell us that it's a bad idea to use the same username and password for different online accounts—if a bad guy cracks your password, he can access your email, bank account, and any other online services associated with that username and password.

That's why it's a good idea to create different usernames and passwords for all accounts. But keeping track of them all is a real task! Fortunately, you can use an app like SafeWallet to secure all your usernames and passwords on your Xoom and never worry about forgetting a password or having it fall into the wrong hands.

1. Search the Android Market for SafeWallet. It costs U.S. $3.99 for the full version.

2. Tap the app to view its information screen and purchase and install it. Open SafeWallet after the installation is complete.

3. The first time you open SafeWallet, the app displays an empty screen with the text No Wallets Found.

4. Tap the Menu button.

5. Tap the New Wallet option.

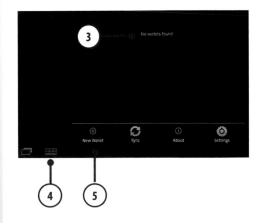

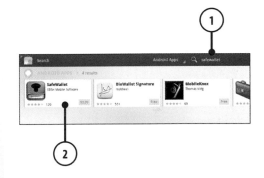

6. Provide a name for your wallet.

7. Type a strong password. If possible, use a combination of upper- and lowercase letters, numerals, and a special character or two (!, #, and $, for example).

8. Re-type the password. And don't forget it! Without this password, you cannot access a wallet, and there is no way to recover a forgotten password with SafeWallet.

9. Tap the Done button to create the storage wallet.

10. Tap a wallet to open it and add some information.

11. Enter the password you created for the wallet.

12. Tap the Done button. The screen displays the contents of the wallet. Each wallet contains Business and Personal folders.

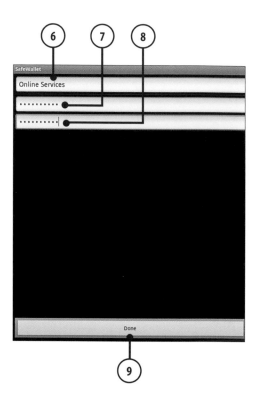

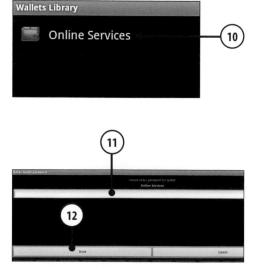

Wallets Defined

SafeWallet enables you to create multiple wallets or you can simply use a single wallet. Think of a wallet as a folder where you store information that includes the name of an account (such as Dropbox), the username (your email address, in the case of Dropbox), and the password…as well as additional information. You can store things such as bank account numbers, Social Security numbers, and more. Using multiple wallets can be useful if you want to keep different types of accounts separate and locked down with a unique password. Because each wallet requires a password to access it, you can easily create a wallet called Online Accounts and another called Financial Accounts—one to hold username and passwords for accessing websites and other online services and the other to contain banking details, credit card numbers, and other data related to your finances.

13. Tap the Menu button.

14. Tap the New Folder button to add a folder to the wallet that you can name.

15. Tap the Personal folder to open it. (Or select a different folder—whichever folder you select will be where a card you create is stored.)

16. Tap the New Card button to add an account and its details, including username, password, and so on.

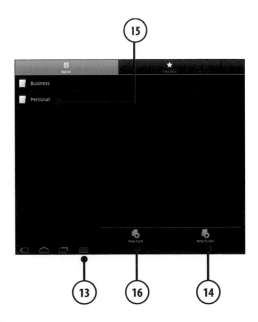

SafeWallet—Not Just for Credit Cards

SafeWallet calls every account you store within its walls a "card." Think of a card as a file that can contain as much or as little information as you choose to provide. For example, if you create a Dropbox card, you would want to include the email address and password to log in. Although most cards you create will only contain a username and password, other cards could hold information you also want secured—Social Security numbers of family members, checking and credit card numbers, a PIN for an ATM card, and more. SafeWallet is also a great way to consolidate all of your secure information for a spouse in case of an emergency— just don't forget to give the wallet password to your spouse!

17. A list of card types appears— scroll through the list to find a suitable description.

18. Tap the card type you want to add to your wallet. (I choose Social Security number.)

19. Provide any or all information requested; you do not have to supply every text field with data, but the more you can provide, the more useful that card might be to you in the future.

20. Tap the Done key to save the card to your wallet.

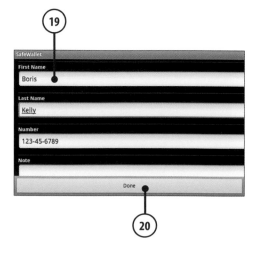

21. Additional card types that you added appear in the list.

22. Tap the Back button twice to return to the list of wallets.

23. Tap a card in the list.

24. The account details are listed.

25. Tap the padlock icon to view the password.

26. The password is now visible.

27. Tap the compass icon to close SafeWallet and open the website in a browser.

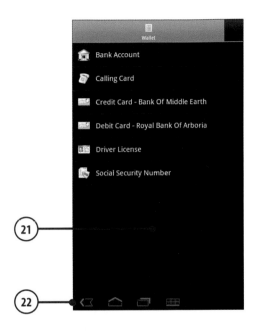

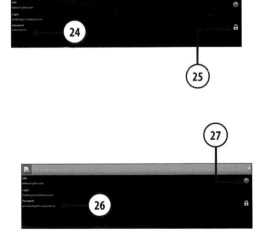

It's Not All Good

CLOSE DOWN SAFEWALLET!

I love the features of SafeWallet, but one thing I don't like is that if you tap Xoom's Home button to run another app and then later reopen the SafeWallet app, the current screen is the one you were last viewing. This means that if you're viewing the cards stored in a wallet, it's still open!

The only way around this is to use the Back button to back out to the list of wallets. From that point, tapping a wallet requires the password to open it. I contacted the app's developer to ask that this be fixed by always forcing the SafeWallet app to return to the wallet list whenever you tap the Home button. For now, you just have to remember to use the Back button.

Watch your home movies, YouTube videos, or box office hits on the Xoom's widescreen compatible display.

In this chapter, you see how easy it is to watch movies on your Xoom and access YouTube, which is the largest online video-upload-and-sharing service around.

15

From the Big Screen to the Small Screen

The Xoom has the perfect screen for watching movies—its dimensions are almost identical to the 16:9 ratio used at movie theaters. However, in addition to watching Hollywood blockbusters, you can also load up your Xoom with home movies of almost all file types (MPEG-4, AVI, and so on) and watch them anytime, anywhere.

In addition to watching movies, your Xoom comes with a free YouTube player app that's been customized to take advantage of the Xoom's touch screen.

Introducing…MoboPlayer

A handful of video-player apps are available for the Xoom; some are free and others are not. They differ in features and how they display movies onscreen, but they all have one thing in common: They require that the movie files be stored on your Xoom.

Fortunately, your Xoom has plenty of storage space, and you'll find that you have room to store a lot of video files. To view all those videos, you need one of these video players. One of the most popular is also 100% free: MoboPlayer. But before you can watch any movies, you need to install the app.

1. Search for MoboPlayer in the Android Market.

2. Tap the app to go to its information page for purchasing and download and installation.

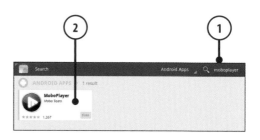

Downloading and Installing Apps

Jump back to Chapter 7, "The Android Market," for instructions on purchasing, downloading, installing, and uninstalling apps. This chapter assumes that you can search the Android Market for the apps mentioned and install and run them from the Apps folder.

3. After installing MoboPlayer, run the app either by tapping the Open button on the app's information page or tapping the MoboPlayer app in the Apps folder.

4. The first time you open MoboPlayer, you see gesture shortcuts on the screen for use while watching a movie.

5. Tap the Pass button.

MoboPlayer Plays Files on the Xoom Only

MoboPlayer is not a movie or TV streaming service like Netflix (www.netflix.com) or Hulu (www.hulu.com). It requires movie files to be stored on the Xoom device itself. If you have a Netflix or Hulu account (or other service), check the company's website for information related to using its services on your Xoom. Be aware that many of these services do not yet support the Xoom.

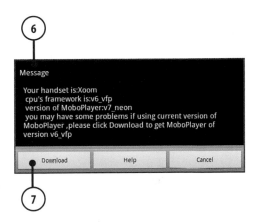

6. You might receive an error message, depending on the version of MoboPlayer that you have downloaded. (This error message might not appear to you, because the problem might be resolved by the time you read this, and you can jump to the next section.)

7. Tap the Download button.

8. You see a Starting Download message—a file is downloaded that updates MoboPlayer and enables it to work on the Xoom.

9. After the update file downloads, tap the Home button to exit any apps (including MoboPlayer).

10. Open the Apps folder and tap the Settings app.

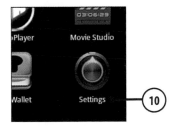

11. Uninstall the MoboPlayer app. Refer to Chapter 7 for instructions on uninstalling apps.

12. Open the Apps folder and tap the Downloads app.

Uninstalling MoboPlayer

The file you downloaded installs a version of MoboPlayer that works on your Xoom, but you must first uninstall the version of MoboPlayer that's already installed.

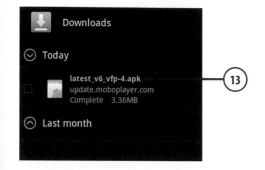

13.   Tap the file latest_v6_vfp-4.apk to open it.

14.   Tap the Install button.

15.   After the installation is complete, tap the Open button.

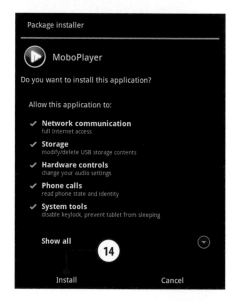

16. Tap the Pass button.

17. Tap Click Here to tell MoboPlayer where to look for movie files.

18. Scroll down the list of folders and tap Movies. Any movie files in the Movies folder are displayed.

19. Tap a movie icon to open and watch the movie. If your folder is empty, it's time to learn how to load it with movies.

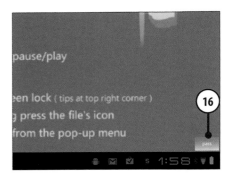

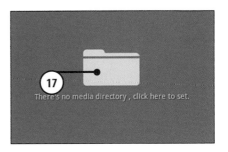

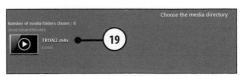

Loading Movies

There's a good chance that you can use MoboPlayer on your Xoom to watch any movie that you have on your computer, whether you recorded it with a video recorder or downloaded it from a website. But before you watch any movie, you need to move it from the computer and into Xoom's storage.

1. Connect your Xoom to your computer or laptop with a USB cable.

2. Tap the Windows Start button.

3. Select Computer.

4. Double-click the Xoom icon.

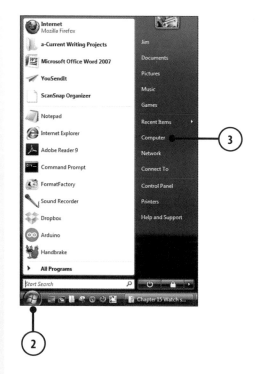

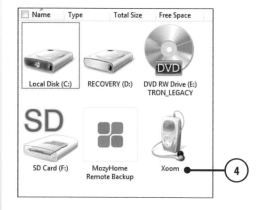

5. Double-click the Device Storage file.

6. Double-click the Movies folder. Copy (or cut and paste) movie files from your computer to this folder.

7. Existing movies in the folder are represented by an icon and the filename (typically the movie title) is displayed. In this example, one movie is currently stored on the Xoom.

8. Copy any movie files that you want to view on your Xoom to the Movies folder.

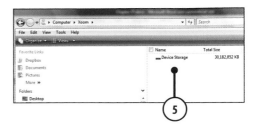

Name	Size	Modified
Alarms		2/18/2011 1:42 AM
Android		2/4/2011 7:45 PM
astrid		3/12/2011 11:47 AN
DCIM		3/19/2011 11:36 AN
Download		3/31/2011 10:41 AN
drocap		3/8/2011 10:24 AM
foursquare		2/24/2011 3:31 PM
glu		3/6/2011 7:11 PM
kindle		3/30/2011 12:49 PN
Movies		2/18/2011 1:42 AM
Music		3/31/2011 10:03 AN
Notifications		2/18/2011 1:42 AM
Pictures		2/18/2011 1:42 AM
Podcasts		2/18/2011 1:42 AM
Ringtones		2/18/2011 1:42 AM
ScreenCaptureLib		3/1/2011 3:11 PM
screenshots		3/18/2011 10:36 AN
TunnyBrowser		4/4/2011 2:29 PM
robo_defense_full.b...	1 KB	3/21/2011 10:56 AN

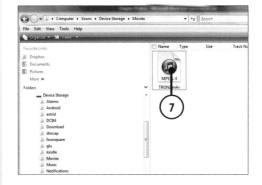

9. I have three different movie formats saved in the Movies folder: mov, wmv, and m4v.

10. After copying all the movie files, close the window on the computer and unplug the Xoom.

11. Open the MoboPlayer app.

12. All the movie files copied are displayed.

13. Tap a movie to watch it.

14. Your selected movie immediately begins to play.

15. Tap the Pause button to pause the movie.

16. Tap the Screen button to toggle between 4:3 (TV) format and 16:9 (widescreen).

17. Tap the Movie List button to return to the previous screen and your list of movies.

18. Tap and hold while dragging left or right to fast forward or rewind the movie.

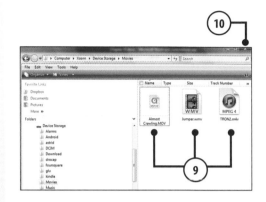

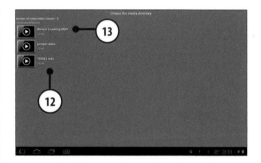

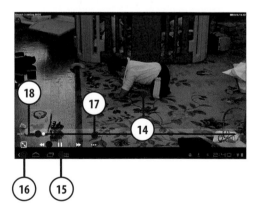

Watching DVD Movies

The Xoom obviously doesn't have the capability to play DVDs, but that doesn't mean you can't watch the DVD movies you've purchased on your Xoom. It's a bit more complicated than simply copying over files such as your home movies, but if you're set on doing it, point your web browser to this online article I wrote that walks you through the process. It involves downloading and installing two free applications on your computer, but the article is easy to follow and, when you're done, you'll know how to convert any DVD movie you own into an M4V file that can be stored and watched on your Xoom. You can find the article at www.quepublishing.com/articles/article.aspx?p=1655237. Note that the article shows how to move the converted file to the iPad—instead of using iTunes, you simply copy that file to your Xoom's Movies folder.

Using YouTube

Everyone is familiar with YouTube—we've all clicked a link to watch some crazy and hilarious video a friend or family member emailed over with a subject line saying, "You've got to watch this!" YouTube is where everyone goes to find amateur video uploaded by people around the world. Some of it is humorous, some of it is educational, and some of it simply cannot be categorized.

Most people access YouTube via a web browser from a computer, but there are apps for most devices, including the Xoom, that allow access to YouTube's online database of videos. Xoom's YouTube app is ready for you to open; it provides a custom interface designed just for the honeycomb operating system.

1. Open the Apps folder and tap the YouTube app to open it.

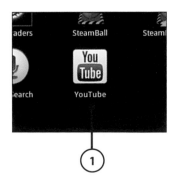

2. Each small screen is a single video that can be played by tapping it.

3. The length of each video is displayed in the lower-left corner of each screen.

4. Videos are selected for the YouTube home screen from the Most Popular, Most Discussed, and Most Viewed ratings.

5. Tap the Browse button.

6. Tap a category that interests you from the list on the left.

7. Related videos appear on the right.

8. Tap the This Week button to filter videos in a category based on when they were uploaded (Today, This Week, This Month, and All Time).

9. Tap the Ratings button to filter videos and view only those that are Top Rated, Top Favorited, Most Viewed, or Most Discussed.

10. Enter text to perform a search to find videos of interest.

11. Tap the Microphone button and say aloud what types of videos you want to view.

12. Tap a video to open it.

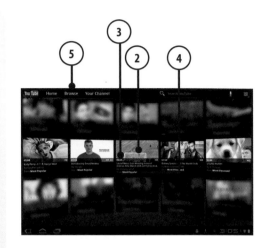

13. The video immediately begins to play.

14. Read details about the video.

15. Related videos appear to the right.

16. Tap on the video for controls to appear.

17. Tap the Pause button to pause the video.

18. Drag the progress dot left or right to rewind or forward through the video.

19. Rate the video with a thumbs up or thumbs down.

20. Tap the username of the video's uploader to view more videos from that user.

21. Tap the Share button to email a link to the video to a friend.

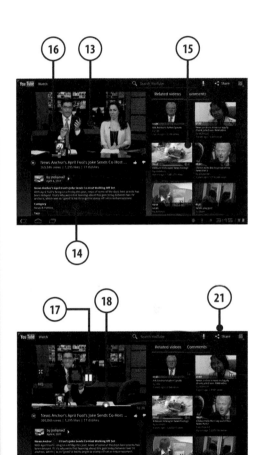

It's Not All Good

TOO MUCH INFORMATION

YouTube can be overwhelming; there is just too much to sift through. That's why using categories and search are so critical. It's estimated that YouTube adds more than 24 hours of video footage every minute. Yes, that's right—every 60 seconds, users upload more than 24 hours of content. You'll never be able to watch it all, so don't even try.

You also want to be careful when opening the YouTube app on your Xoom when in public places. Some video titles and thumbnails that appear on the screen can be offensive. YouTube has few limits on what can be uploaded, so treat YouTube as a Wild West of sorts and be careful where you tap.

And remember that your Xoom also has that HDMI slot for connecting to a larger screen. Simply use an HDMI cable to connect your Xoom to your flatscreen TV or other display (with HDMI input), and you can watch YouTube videos on a larger screen.

Thousands of apps are available that give your Xoom features and capabilities that don't fall into any particular category.

In this chapter, you are introduced to some of the many apps that are either hard to categorize or so complex that they'd almost require their own chapter or book. These are only introductions, so you need to download, install, and experiment with them to learn all the available features.

16

→ Vendetta

→ Mint.com

→ AllRecipes.com Dinner Spinner

→ Google Sky Map

→ ESPN ScoreCenter

→ Seek Droid

Apps, Apps, and More Apps

One of the best things about Xoom apps is how inexpensive most of them are—and that's not counting the thousands and thousands of apps that are 100% free! Typically, for less than a few dollars, you can download an app that interests you and not risk losing a lot of money if you find that the app just doesn't meet your needs. (If you can determine that in less than 15 minutes, you even get a refund for most apps.)

Even the apps that cost more are still less than most software you find for your computer, meaning that you can load up your Xoom with dozens of apps for less than the price of the average software box (usually around $30–40).

There is simply no way to cover every app that you can grab from the Android Market. However, in this chapter, you find a nice summary of some amazing apps, along with some screenshots that give you a good idea of what to expect. These apps are scattered over all the categories of the Android Market—Games, Productivity, Business, Education, Finance, and more.

If you can, develop a habit of checking the Android Market every day or at least once a week. Start scanning the featured apps and the best-selling apps—the apps listed there are typically those that many other Xoom users find useful, fun, educational, and often simply must-have apps.

Vendetta

Vendetta is a game that started growing in popularity even before it was released. The game was featured in an early television commercial for the Xoom tablet and featured a user grabbing the Xoom and having it morph into a spaceship that surrounded the user and dropped him right into the heat of an epic space battle.

Vendetta is a complex game—you play against other players around the world. As the captain of your own spaceship, you fight battles, mine asteroids, barter with merchants, chase pirates, and more. However, all of this comes at a price! Vendetta is a subscription-based game that sets you back $10 a month to participate. But what a game it is! If you're looking for one of the most cutting-edge games with some of the best graphics, music, and sound effects, download the app and try it for 16 hours absolutely free.

1. Install the app and any updates—the app automatically updates itself.

2. Tap the Demo or Tutorial button to learn how to play, including how to fly your ship, fight bad guys, and more.

3. Tap the Play button to start your free 16-hour trial. You create a username and password and are required to log in every time you want to play.

4. Tap the Help button to visit the official Vendetta website and read the online manual.

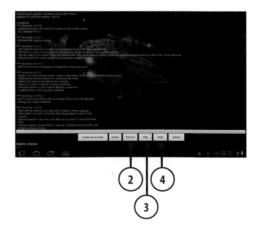

5. After you tap Play, the Vendetta online game begins.

6. Log in with your username and password every time you want to play.

7. Tap the Connect button to begin.

8. Create your character by tapping a Create a New Character button. You can have up to six characters, so create a good guy, a pirate, a merchant, and more. Each character enables you to behave differently. The pirate is fun when you're feeling a bit dastardly. I created my first pilot named The Bookworm.

9. Tap Events and News to keep up to date with the game.

10. After creating a character, tap Play, and get ready.

11. You get to create and customize the look of your ship.

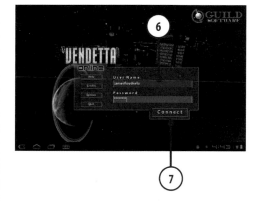

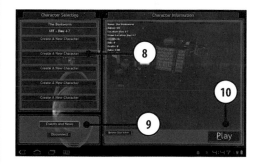

12.   Mine an asteroid for rare ores…

13.   …or pick a fight by opening up your weapons on an enemy!

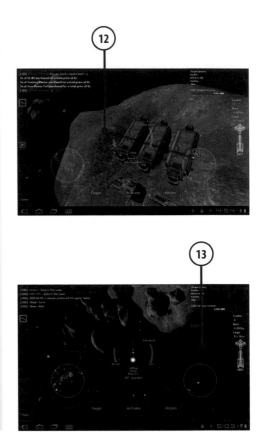

Mint.com

Mint.com is a browser-based financial-management tool that enables you to view all of your financial accounts: checking, savings, investments, and more. It's a handy service for pulling in all of your records and accessing them with a single Mint.com login.

The Mint.com app that runs on Xoom has a simple interface; you log in and then "link" your accounts to the Mint.com app. To link an account, you need to provide the username and password that you use to access these accounts separately (such as an ID and password for your online checking service).

Mint.com has strong security, but even then, the information displayed on the app is only for viewing; you cannot transfer funds, make purchases, or close accounts. If someone is able to crack your Mint.com account, the only thing he could do is view your financial data; not good in itself, but you won't find your checking account emptied.

The Mint.com app is a free download from Intuit and requires that you create a Mint.com account before using the app. You can create this account on the Xoom or on a computer by accessing www.mint.com. (Although the current app is designed for mobile phones—thus the smaller screen—there are plans to release a customized version for tablet users.)

1. You must log in every time you run the Mint.com app.

2. You're given an immediate summary of your cash on hand.

3. Credit card debt is listed.

4. Tap to view more details.

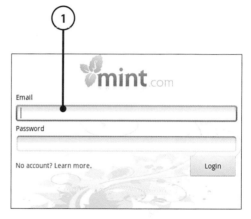

5. Green indicates an investment or cash on hand or savings.

6. Black indicates a debt.

7. Create and view your budget and its expenditures.

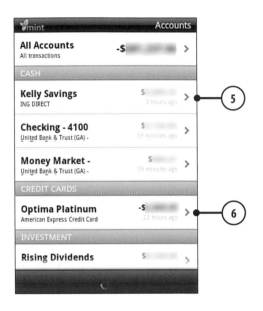

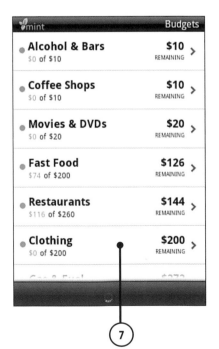

8. You can drill down to see spending in various categories, such as books or online book stores.

9. Alerts are useful for spotting unusual activity.

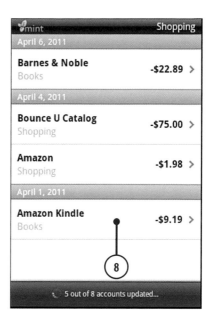

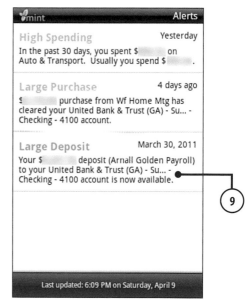

AllRecipes.com Dinner Spinner

It doesn't matter if you like to cook or hate to cook. If you like to cook, you will greet the Dinner Spinner as a welcome source of new recipes. If you don't like to cook, the Dinner Spinner will help you get meals created faster and easier.

The app can work randomly, like a slot machine—you pull the lever and Dinner Spinner picks a random dish, random ingredients, and a preparation/cooking time and then provides you with any matches it finds in its extensive database of recipes.

However, the app also enables you to specify exactly what you're looking for, so you can pick appetizer, three or four key ingredients that you have in your cupboard or fridge, and then select a "20 minutes or less" prep time to view matches.

Recipes come with ratings from other Dinner Spinner users, detailed instructions for preparing, and often, great photos of the final product.

The AllRecipes.com Dinner Spinner is a free app that you can download and install from the Android Market.

1. After downloading the app, launch it. The Dinner Spinner app has a unique interface.

2. Dish types are displayed on the top row.

3. Ingredients are displayed on the middle row.

4. Prep/cooking time options appear on the bottom row.

5. Tap the Spin Categories button for a totally random selection.

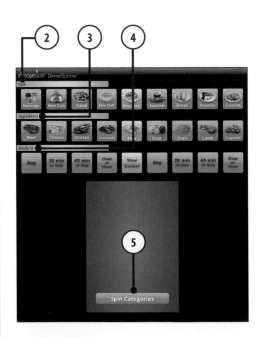

6. The random options that are picked appear in blue.

7. Tap View Matches to see any recipes that exist.

8. Recipes are listed along with a photo (if one exists).

9. Reviews (based on 1–5 stars) are provided.

10. Tap a recipe to view its ingredients and directions.

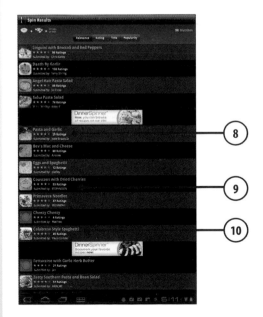

11. View the ingredients.

12. Read over the directions to prepare the dish.

13. Tap to view more details related to nutritional data.

14. Tap to read reviews from other users.

15. You can also tap buttons on the Dinner Spinner main menu to select items rather than allow a random selection.

16. Tap Soup/Stew on the Dish row.

17. Tap Fish on the Ingredients row.

18. Tap Slow Cooker on the Ready In row.

19. Tap the View Matches button.

20. There are three options for Soup/Stew with fish as an ingredient and slow cooked!

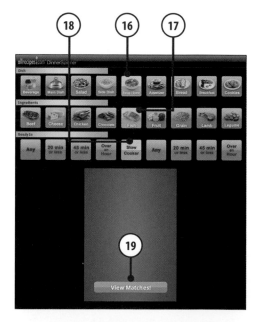

Google Sky Map

Google Sky Map is simply one of the apps that you just have to see to believe. It uses the built-in GPS capabilities and the built-in compass sensor (for tilt detection) of your Xoom to assist you with finding planets, stars, and constellations. It obviously works best outside and at night, but it's not required.

You simply hold the Xoom in both hands and move it around in space. The onscreen display changes to show you the approximate location of stars and planets. Constellations are easy to spot because Sky Map draws their outlines onscreen to assist you with finding the right stars.

The horizon is also represented by a solid line. Any stars or planets below that line are obviously out of your line of sight, but you can still see what's in the sky and what others are seeing in other parts of the world.

1. Open Google Sky Maps; outside is best.

2. At first, a random portion of the sky appears. Allow Sky Maps to calibrate its location using GPS.

3. The horizon is represented by a solid line running left to right.

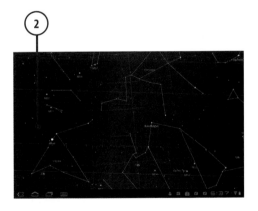

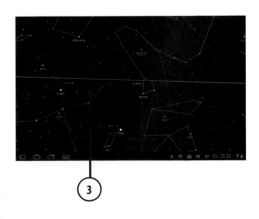

4. Hold the Xoom so that it is angled up (pointing above the horizon). Stand as still as possible and try to keep the Xoom from moving.

5. Stars, planets, and constellations that are behind the Xoom are displayed.

6. Tap the Menu button.

7. Select Toggle Night Mode.

8. The Xoom's screen is dimmed and stars, planets, and constellations appear in red. (This is better for night vision.)

9. Tap the Menu button and select Toggle Night Mode to toggle the screen back to Normal viewing mode.

10. Tap anywhere onscreen.

11. You can toggle on and off items such as stars, planets, and constellation outlines by tapping their respective buttons.

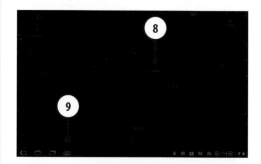

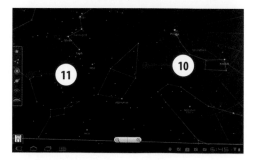

ESPN ScoreCenter

Whether you only follow one team or a dozen, ESPN ScoreCenter is a customizable app that enables you to quickly view those games and/or teams that are important to you. With a quick swipe on the screen, you can blaze through all the various sporting events that are in season and read up-to-the-minute sports reporting.

While a game is in play, you can zoom into the details, getting play-by-play stats and commentary as it happens. This makes the ScoreCenter app a great app for taking with you to a game. And with so many sports facilities offering Wi-Fi to their patrons, you'll likely be able to view real-time video without worrying about data limits.

ESPN ScoreCenter is a free app from the Android Market.

1. After installing ScoreCenter, open the app.

2. ScoreCenter opens to the myTeams page. Here, you can specify a mix of sports, teams, and leagues and have their latest scores displayed.

3. Tap the + button to browse through a list of sports.

4. Teams you selected to follow appear on the page.

5. Upcoming games are displayed along with the opponent, date, and time.

6. Tap the Selection button to select from seven available sports.

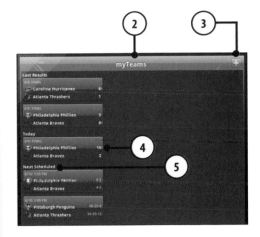

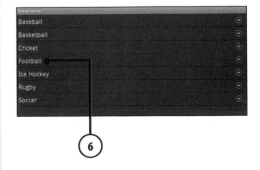

7. Use the Selection button to burrow into leagues or divisions (includes college and professional for most sports).

8. Select a team to add.

9. The team you select is added to your myTeams page.

10. Tap to scroll through the various other pages offered.

11. View the latest sporting event summaries.

12. Tap a game to view more details.

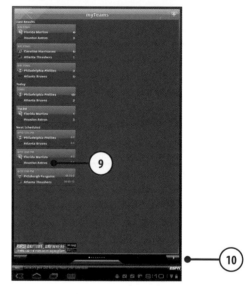

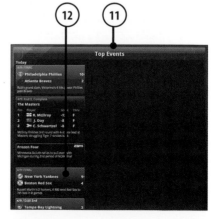

13. View the details of the game.

14. Tap Recap to read a detailed summary.

15. Read the game recap.

16. Tap for stats on individual players.

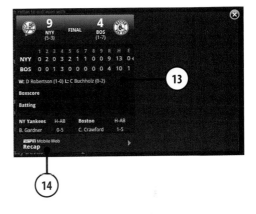

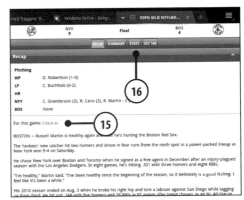

Seek Droid

If you have a tendency to misplace items such as your keys or your mobile phone, the thought of losing your Xoom probably fills you with dread. Fortunately, there's an inexpensive solution that can give you some peace of mind.

Seek Droid is a $0.99 app. If your Xoom is ever lost or stolen, this app could very well help you locate it, making it one of the cheapest forms of insurance on your tablet that you can get.

1. After purchasing, downloading, and installing the app, open the Seek Droid app.

2. Follow the onscreen instructions to register as a new user and log in.

3. Activate the Seek Droid administrator, which allows the app to remotely erase all data (should it be stolen), lock the screen, and change the password.

4. Tap the Menu button to access the main menu and perform various activities.

5. Tap to disable the capability for Seek Droid to lock your device and/or delete all data.

6. Verify the app is registered and then close it. Your Xoom is registered with the SeekDroid.com website.

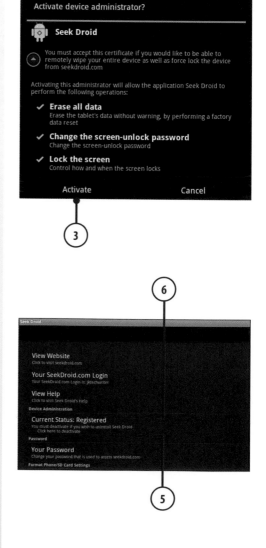

7. If your Xoom is lost or stolen, open a web browser on a computer and visit www.seekdroid.com.

8. Log in to the seekdroid.com website with your username and password.

9. If the Xoom is turned on, seekdroid.com attempts to locate it using GPS.

10. If the Xoom is located, and it's not where you can retrieve it or it's in someone else's possession, tap the Wipe button to delete all data.

11. Tap the Lock button to lock the Xoom with a new password. This prevents a thief from unlocking the Xoom and accessing your data, but don't forget your new password or you will be unable to unlock it as well.

12. Tap the Alarm button to trigger an audible alarm that plays through the Xoom's speakers. It's useful for finding your Xoom (look under the couch) as well as annoying any thief who currently has your Xoom. The alarm can only be turned off by entering the new password you created when you tapped the Lock button.

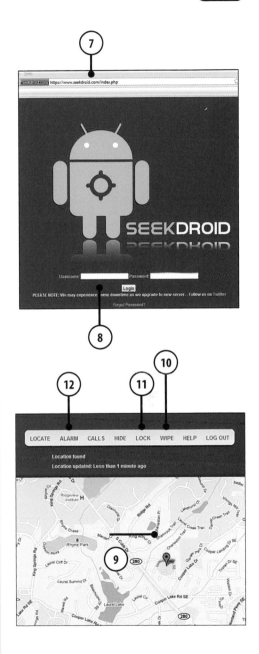

Xoom accessories can make using your tablet more enjoyable as well as protect it from damage and ensure the battery never dies.

In this chapter, you learn about the handful of Xoom accessories available that can protect your Xoom, make it easier to type, enable you to use your Xoom to listen to music and watch videos on a larger screen, and keep your Xoom charged while you're on the go.

17

→ Case Protection

→ Charging Stations

→ External Keyboard

→ Car Charger

→ USB Port

Accessories Make Life Easier

With Xoom in its infancy, the options are somewhat limited right now when it comes to accessories, but don't expect that to last.

Even today, however, there are a small number of useful accessories that can improve your experience with the Xoom.

Case Protection

Unless you are in the habit of only using your Xoom while sitting on the couch with a heavy shag carpet under your feet and plenty of pillows surrounding you, you need a case for your Xoom. You already invested a nice sum of cash on your new tablet, so give serious consideration to spending just a few more dollars to protect it from spills and short falls. (I said short, because I'm not aware of any case that can protect your Xoom from a drop of more than a few feet.)

A case keeps the screen covered and, let's face it, a nice case just looks better than carrying the device, unprotected, around in public.

Cases are one of those items that manufacturers have already raced to provide, so you have a nice selection from which to choose.

You can go with the official Motorola Portfolio Case, which offers good protection and a nice folding feature that enables you to prop up your Xoom on a desk for easier viewing.

Official Motorola Accessories

To view all the available Motorola accessories (and new ones that are not yet released), go to www.motorola.com and use the search feature to search for "Xoom Accessories." You'll find them all with nice photos and detailed writeups.

For a more comprehensive list of Xoom cases, go to Amazon.com to find quite a few more options. Search for "Motorola Xoom Case."

My Xoom is protected by the black leather Executive Folio from Kiwi Cases. It's not fancy, but it didn't cost me a fortune, and four elastic bands hold the corners snug and the screen is well protected.

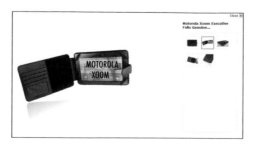

Executive Folio

You can search Amazon.com for the Executive Folio for Xoom or simply use this URL: www.amazon.com/gp/product/B004NJVUTY.

Again, if you value your Xoom and want to keep it clean and somewhat protected, get a case. It's a small cost compared to the repair charge you might get from a spill or fall.

Charging Stations

Currently, Motorola offers two different charging stations for the Xoom. You can always charge your Xoom with the included AC adapter, but these charging stations offer more functionality than simply charging the Xoom's battery.

The first charging station is the Standard Dock.

The Standard Dock holds the Xoom at a nice viewing angle while it charges. With it, you can also plug in a pair of external speakers; the Xoom's own speakers (on the back) are okay, but they're not going to really be able to broadcast speech and music.

One downside to the Standard Dock is that, while the Xoom is docked and charging, access to the HDMI port is blocked. This means that you cannot use an HDMI cable to connect your Xoom to a large LCD TV, for example. For that functionality, you'll want to investigate the Speaker Dock.

The Speaker Dock is a slightly larger charging station. It holds the Xoom at a slightly greater angle than the Standard Dock, but it does have an HDMI port on the back that enables you to connect your Xoom to an external display (such as a TV or larger computer screen) using an HDMI cable.

The Speaker Dock also comes with a pair of built-in speakers that provide a higher volume than the Xoom's standard built-in speakers.

Both docks are great for using your Xoom to listen to music (whether you're listening to your own MP3 files or using a music service, such as Pandora) while charging at the same time. You can watch movies and video while the Xoom is docked on either station, but if you intend to watch full-length movies from your Xoom, definitely consider getting the Speaker Dock versus the Standard Dock, simply for the HDMI output capability.

External Keyboard

Entering information such as your name, password, or website URLs is fine with the onscreen keyboard. It's not a great solution, but you're not exactly writing a novel, either.

If you intend to do any kind of writing on your Xoom, however—either with a note or word processing app—investigate the Motorola Wireless Keyboard.

The wireless keyboard connects to your Xoom via Bluetooth. Not only does it provide a full-size keyboard for typing with your Xoom, but it also has short-cut keys that you can use instead of onscreen menu buttons, such as Home or Back.

Combine the wireless keyboard with the Speaker Dock and an HDMI cable connecting your Xoom to a large LCD TV, and you have a serious setup for web browsing, watching movies, and using apps (especially those that require entering text)!

Car Charger

The final accessory for you to consider is the Motorola Car Charger. The car charger plugs into the cigarette lighter and provides the same adapter end found on your standard Xoom charger.

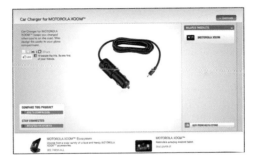

If you're like me and take your Xoom wherever you go, you've likely encountered the low battery pop-up warning. I typically don't carry my standard Xoom AC adapter charger with me, so having the car charger means that I can keep it plugged in while I drive, enabling me to use the GPS navigation capability and not get lost while in an unknown town.

USB Port

The micro-USB port on the bottom of your Xoom (right next to the HDMI port) might not seem at first to be an accessory, but think about it: How many accessories do you have for your computer or laptop that plug into a free USB port?

There's the printer…and my portable scanner…and my external hard drive…and my video camera…and the list goes on.

With that single USB port on your Xoom, device manufacturers have the ability to offer Xoom owners a range of services and devices that can be plugged in and used. If you have a device that you enjoy using on your home computer, consider contacting the manufacturer and asking what it would take for that company to create an app that allows a Xoom user to plug in the device. It never hurts to ask, and you might find a familiar accessory for your computer now working with your Xoom.

Index

X–Z

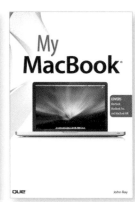

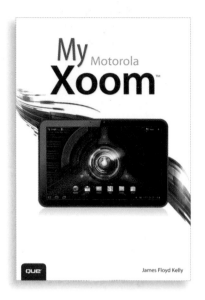

My Motorola Xoom™

James Floyd Kelly

que

FREE Online Edition

Your purchase of **My Motorola Xoom™** includes access to a free online edition for 45 days through the Safari Books Online subscription service. Nearly every Que book is available online through Safari Books Online, along with more than 5,000 other technical books and videos from publishers such as Addison-Wesley Professional, Cisco Press, Exam Cram, IBM Press, O'Reilly, Prentice Hall, and Sams.

SAFARI BOOKS ONLINE allows you to search for a specific answer, cut and paste code, download chapters, and stay current with emerging technologies.

Activate your FREE Online Edition at www.informit.com/safarifree

> **STEP 1:** Enter the coupon code: IWLAOVH.

> **STEP 2:** New Safari users, complete the brief registration form.
> Safari subscribers, just log in.

If you have difficulty registering on Safari or accessing the online edition,
please e-mail customer-service@safaribooksonline.com